The Artisans and Guilds of France

Beautiful Craftsmanship Through the Centuries

By François Icher

Translated from the French
by John Goodman

Harry N. Abrams, Inc., Publishers

To Marie, Guillaume, and Julien

Editor, English-language edition: Julia Gaviria
Design Coordinators, English-language edition: Dirk Luykx and Tina Thompson

Library of Congress Catalog Card Number: 99–68521
ISBN 0–8109–4390–5

Printed and bound in Spain

Harry N. Abrams, Inc.
100 Fifth Avenue
New York, N.Y. 10011
www.abramsbooks.com

Contents

n 1901, in his book *Le compagnonnage, son histoire, ses coutumes, ses règlements et ses rites* (*Compagnonnage:* its history, customs, rules, and rites), the historian Étienne Martin Saint-Léon predicted the rapid disappearance of all journeyman confraternities: "*Compagnonnage* is now almost unknown to the public, and its very name is slowly disappearing from popular memory. . . . *Compagnonnage* is dead or dying. It no longer has more than an almost insignificant number of members. Its recruitment sources have fallen silent. . . . Only a few green branches still flourish at the top of the ancient tree, whose sap is receding and whose trunk will not much longer prove resistant to storms." Saint-Léon's attitude was shared by most of his contemporaries: at a time when the world of labor was undergoing the most profound transformations in its history due to advancing mechanization, capitalism, and syndicalism, journeyman confraternities were experiencing a crisis thought to be fatal. But given that the crafts for which such organizations existed had somehow avoided their predicted demise, a number of observers acknowledged their mistake. Even Saint-Léon modified his pessimistic assessment in 1927 in a special issue of the periodical *Le Voile d'Isis*, where he advanced a somewhat different view under the evocative title "The Future of *Compagnonnage*."

Yet again, *compagnonnage* had emerged victorious from a battle that it had seemed fated to lose. Here we come to a key point that, in part, defines this workers' institution, which has managed, over a history encompassing more than six centuries, to survive persecution, bans, crises, revolution, and war. To follow in the footsteps of journeymen on the famous voyage of training and socialization known as the Tour de France is to discover a workers' movement that has survived thanks to its remarkable ability to adapt to changing political, economic, and social contexts. Faced with the condemnation of French kings and the church, the *devoirs* (as such confraternities are known) of past eras always responded by organizing groups that were structured, courageous, and generous, articulated around the Tour de France. United by hope and determined self-promotion, the multitude of workers knew they would be lost if yoked to the corporations or guilds of the Old Regime. Regulations, decrees, and monitories never managed to deter an ever-growing number of youth from benefiting from the privileges offered by the various journeyman organizations. Even in troubled periods of war, the *devoirs* recruited large numbers of young men lured by an extraordinary journey and by the prospect of acceptance into a new family that was extremely solicitous of its members' interests.

To focus only on journeyman culture of ancient times would be an error for those who share their love for its contemporary manifestations. In fact, it is worth examining the evolution of the two *compagnonnages*. There was the early Tour de France on foot, in which itinerant workmen traveled from chapter house to chapter house, learning a craft and meeting fellow craftsmen. This was the time of a certain folklore, in which customs and rituals figured prominently in the lives of various journeyman members; a moment when the notion of beautiful work did not run afoul of the pitiless laws of the market. From the time of the cathedrals to that of the first automobiles, *compagnonnage* scarcely modified its political outlook based on a "family" of craftsmen venerating manual skill and craft secrets. World Wars I and II accelerated a process already under way in the early years of the twentieth century. More than a regeneration or renovation, contemporary *compagnonnage* has wedded with the norms of modern society. In this sense, today's journeymen rightly see themselves as profoundly rooted in the modern world even as they remain attached to the legacy of the elders. Thus tradition and innovation coexist harmoniously within the various societies that constitute the modern French landscape of *compagnonnage*.

So it is in these two surprisingly complementary forms of organization that *compagnonnage* summons us in this exploration through time, place, and craft traditions. We evoke both past and present as we undertake a virtual Tour de France, which aims to encompass as much as possible the different itineraries of yesterday and today. Although we must narrow our focus to certain towns for purposes of space, this view of *compagnonnage* is meant to be free of partisan bias. From Chartres to Tours, this voyage through the realm of journeyman culture passes through sixteen cities full of rich traditions. From Jerusalem to Orléans, by way of Sainte-Baume in Provence, we will encounter the myths and legends that clarify the essence of the venerable workers' institution. Along the way, we will profile each of the three current French journeyman organizations. And to conclude our virtual Tour de France, we will examine the principal crafts that have shaped the daily realities as well as the ideals of French journeymen, the authentic guardians not only of an ideology but of a true workers' spirit.

MYTHS AND LEGENDS

ompagnonnage claims three legendary founders: Solomon, Master Jacques, and Father Soubise. As they are allegorical figures, all the texts and stories recounting their involvement in the construction of the Temple in Jerusalem, the project that ostensibly led to the establishment of the order of journeymen, must be decoded. Other sites, periods, and persons also figure in the legends associated with the fellowship, and they, too, should be considered in order to better understand the character of the institution.

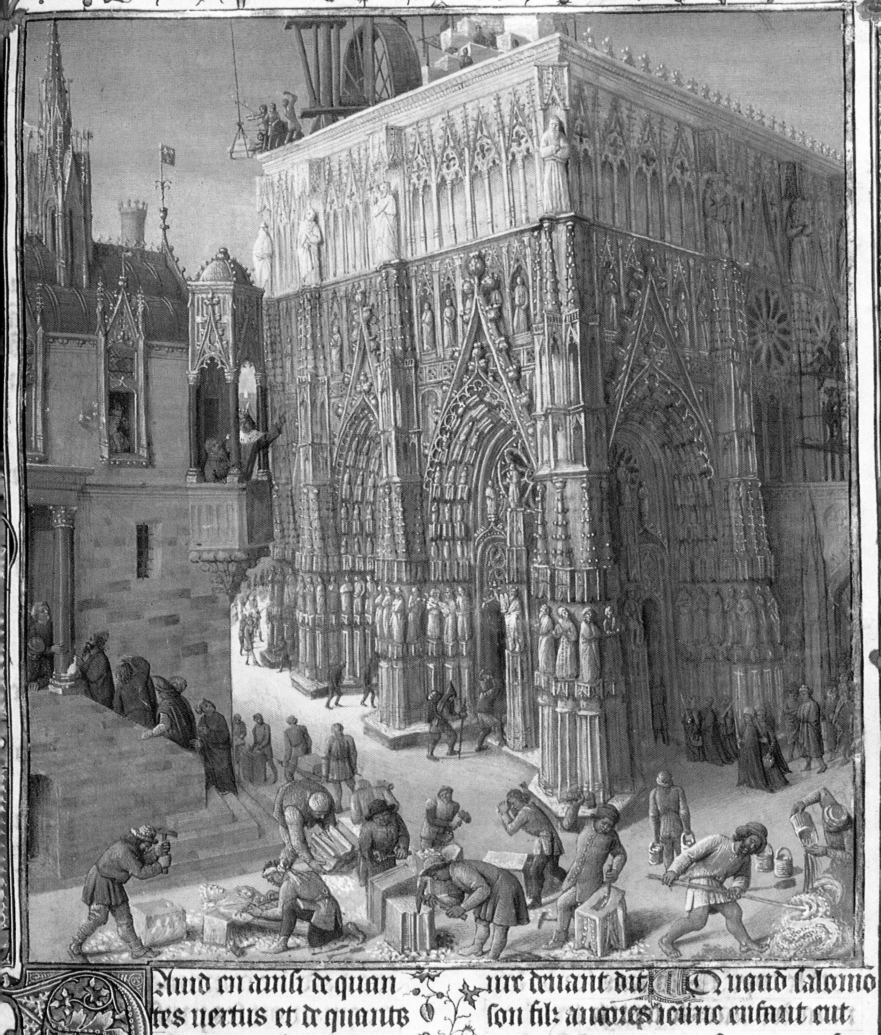

Quand en ainsi de quan   uire deuant dit   Quand salomo
tes uertus et de quantz   son filz: encores iceune enfant eut
biens il a este aucteur   pzins le royaume de son pere. et ka
a ceulx de sa lignee. et   assis ou siege royal. tout le peuple
combien plain de grant aage il est   solennelment faueur. comme on

Jerusalem, or the Mythic Birth of the *Devoir*

onstruction of the Temple
To understand the fellowship and its emergence and development as well as its organization over the centuries, we must turn first to the historical record. But a historical approach alone will prove inadequate for understanding the institution's very essence. In fact, scholars specializing in the history of journeyman culture have always been careful to stress the importance of the many myths and legends that recount, in rich detail, the foundation of the fellowship at the moment when King Solomon summoned a multitude of laborers to Jerusalem to build a sacred edifice, a Temple to the Almighty. It is worth noting that although the Bible recounts Solomon's building project in Jerusalem, *The Book of Kings* makes no mention of anything remotely similar to the fellowship of journeymen.

King Solomon and Master Hiram

According to some legends, King Solomon was aided by an architect named Hiram, a famous master of the art of metalworking. A great work-site organizer, Hiram soon realized the necessity of enforcing discipline on the thousands of men from various countries engaged in so many different tasks. First, it was necessary to assess the quality of their work and to pay them accordingly, as well as to expose idlers who, profiting from the confusion, were being remunerated without cause. Thus Hiram (or Solomon) established an order of journeymen-builders of the Temple, a hierarchical organization open only to those who met strict entry requirements. When a worker had demonstrated the requisite degree of competence, he was led to a room below the Temple where, before the assembled membership, Hiram inducted him and transmitted to him various passwords and signs of recognition that he could use to signal his membership in the order. According to these legends, the fellowship was born in the tenth century B.C., in the Middle East:

> When Solomon, Master Jacques, and Soubise
> Built for the Lord in ancient days,
> In Palestine, an eternal church
> Where everything shone with brilliance and splendor
> These great works brought our masters,

Throughout the universe, an immortal renown.
The sanctuary of those days saw the birth
Of the sacred order of noble journeymen.
—"Le Blason," nineteenth-century song by Paul Calas,
known as *Languedocien l'Ami des Filles*
(The friend to young women from Languedoc)

Hiram was assassinated by three disgruntled workers who had been refused initiation into the mysteries of the order; his body was placed in a bronze tomb. His assassins were later discovered and severely tortured. Solomon then changed the passwords and signs of recognition.

Hiram first appears in the fellowship legends rather late. In the traditional language of the order, there has never been any question of the "children of Hiram": its songs honor only the followers of Solomon, Master Jacques, and Soubise. The *devoir de liberté* seems to be the source of this popular legend of Hiram, which arose between the late eighteenth and early nineteenth centuries when the influence of freemasonry became particularly strong in the chapter houses of the *gavots* and the *indiens* (members of different journeyman groups) before being taken up by other *devoirs*, as evidenced by the rituals used by various journeyman organizations during the period. In any case, the story of King Solomon and his assassinated architect forms the mythic foundation of the journeymen of the *devoir de liberté*, whose members, even today, are known as "children of Solomon."

The journeyman legends are not limited to the Solomon-Hiram pairing. Although there are many detailed accounts (similar to those among the freemasons) of the construction of the Temple overseen by a great architect and a great king, two other essential figures appear with them, fostering more complex symbolic and allegorical readings of the stories in which they play a role.

Master Jacques

The figure of Master Jacques is especially important in the society of journeymen long known as the *Saint-Devoir de Dieu* (sacred duty to God). Here again, several diverse accounts describe this founding figure, who holds particular interest for mythographers.

According to the most common legend, Master Jacques was one of Solomon's architects and a colleague of Master Hiram. Born in the fictional town of Carte (a name probably derived from *quatre* [four], identified with matter), young Jacques, it is claimed, taught other children to carve stone. At age fifteen, he traveled to Greece, Egypt, and Palestine before arriving in Jerusalem at age thirty-six. He then took part in the construction of the Temple, erecting, notably, two twelve-sided columns on which he carved various Old Testament scenes as well as a few episodes from his own life. He was named by Solomon (or Hiram) master of the stonecutters, joiners, and masons.

After the Temple was completed, Jacques left Judea in the company of another master, Soubise, with whom he quarreled during their westward passage. Soubise disembarked at Bordeaux and Jacques at Marseilles (in fact, neither city yet existed), both accompanied by a few disciples they had trained in Jerusalem. For three years, Master Jacques traveled the country, often having to protect himself from the disciples of Soubise, who tried to kill him. He finally withdrew to Provence, settling in the hills of Sainte-Baume. It is here that he was stabbed five times with a dagger, betrayed by one of his followers. Before dying, he asked his companions to take an oath of fidelity to God and Sacred Duty. After he had drawn his last breath, his "children" distributed his clothing amongst themselves. The hatters received his cap, the stonecutters his tunic, the locksmiths his sandals, the joiners his mantle, the carpenters his belt, and the wheelwrights his staff. The presence of carpenters on this list is surprising, for, according to the same legends, they could only be children of Soubise. Jacques's remains were solemnly transported by the journeymen to a site near Saint-Maximin, where they were interred after the usual rites.

A second, quite different legend is also associated with Master Jacques. It identifies him as Jacques de Molay, the last grand master of the order of the Temple, who was burned alive on the orders of Philip the Fair. The Templars, who were great builders, were initiated into certain practices and skills that Jacques de Molay had revealed to the masons, stonecutters, and carpenters who worked on the Temple. Societies of journeymen were thus established. This hypothesis, for which there is no historical evidence, is based merely on conjecture. In addition to the traditional building crafts, it is clear that

Opposite: **Illustration from a thirteenth-century Bible showing construction of the Temple of Jerusalem, Amiens**

Right and below: **Stained-glass windows representing Solomon, Jacques, and Soubise commissioned for the Musée de Compagnonnage in Tours by Pierre Petit, known as *Tourangeau le Disciple de la Lumière* (The Disciple of Light from Touraine), journeyman glazier of the Devoirs Unis**

These depictions of the three founding fathers of *compagnonnage* incorporate attributes relating to the various affiliations of the fellowship: biblical and sacred (Solomon), chivalric (Jacques), and monastic (Soubise). There are also allusions to the three fundamental building materials: iron, stone, and wood.

the Templars must have turned to a genius and to some supervisory figure. Thus, besides the traditional wood and metal crafts, there figured farriers, blacksmiths, and harness makers, all of which were necessary to the proper functioning of the Crusade expeditions. Indeed, the Crusades seem to have provided a splendid opportunity for introducing Solomon and the Temple of Jerusalem into journeyman legend. A *devoir* active outside France (the *devoir étranger*) was invented and, as with the followers of Jacques, it was independent of the jurisdiction of the Templars. This may explain the link between Jacques and Solomon. But mythographers must be careful when attempting to explain the complex erection of the Temple that is the corpus of fellowship legend.

Finally, a third version identifies Master Jacques as Jacques Moler, one of the superintendents overseeing construction of Orléans's Cathedral of the Holy Cross and a hero of another famous episode in journeyman legend: the schism of Orléans. This important story is discussed in a later chapter.

Father Soubise

The characterization of Soubise is always dependent on that of Jacques. As we have seen, Soubise was an architect on the construction site in Jerusalem responsible for overseeing the carpenters. Jealous of Jacques's authority, he quarreled with him during their return trip and, according to some versions of the story, even tried to have him assassinated. Another legend identifies Soubise with a Benedictine monk who supposedly helped Jacques Moler build the Cathedral of the Holy Cross in Orléans. In all present journeyman chapter houses, Father Soubise is shown wearing a rough serge robe, as a monk holding a carpenter's compass and unfurling a scroll on which is written, "Always think, work, make progress, serve your neighbor, be modest." Whether monk or architect or

Above: **Miniature from *Bible of Velislav*, c. 1350, National Library, Prague. The Tower of Babel also figures in journeyman symbolism.**

Right: **Print from a collection of journeyman imagery, 1850. Master Jacques was sometimes associated with Jacques de Molay, last grand master of the Templars, who was burned alive by Philip the Fair.**

both, of the three legendary founders of the fellowship, Father Soubise incontestably remains the most mysterious.

From Temple to Cathedral

The Temple of Jerusalem, then, was the mythic point of origin of the order of journeymen. Even today, depictions of the three founders can be found in every chapter house. Songs continue to praise their talents and merits. Induction rituals still honor them.

On reviewing the different legends, it is difficult to distinguish between historic myth and reality regarding the existence of a fellowship of journeymen. Solomon, Jacques, and Soubise represent different facets of the fellowship. According to some, the fellowship's origins are biblical, chivalric, and monastic. For others, Solomon evokes the Near-Eastern tradition of royal art, while Jacques and Soubise embody the Western and Christian branch. It is not surprising, then, that two great buildings function as basic points of reference in these myths of origin: the Temple of Jerusalem and the cathedral of Orléans. Thus, from Near East to West, *compagnonnage* has woven a history filled with legend that does not offer a definite explanation for its emergence. It is clear that an institution was established that safeguards the rich heritage affiliated with every craft fellowship, even those dating from the Middle Ages.

Above: **Strasbourg Cathedral.**
**Cathedrals became major symbols
of the fellowship of journeymen,
whose members claimed a direct
lineage from the medieval
builders' confraternities.**

Left: **Print from a collection of
journeyman imagery**, 1850

LE S^T DEVOIR DE D: E.D.M. J:

LE MONT-MORIA.

LE MONT LIBAN.

MARSEILLE.

LA Ste BAUME.

ORLEANS.

LA LOIRE.

Orléans, or the Schism of the *Devoirs*

Above: **Cathedral at Orléans**

Opposite: **Lithograph depicting Master Jacques, founder of the journeymen of the *devoir*. One of the six vignettes behind him pictures the schism of the *devoirs* in Orléans.**

onstruction of the Sainte-Croix

Another important page in the legendary history of the fellowship of journeymen is set in Orléans, where the now famous episode of the schism of the *devoirs* took place. Accounts date the episode to 1401, during construction of the towers of the Cathedral of the Holy Cross. Work was overseen by Jacques Moler, known as *La Flèche d'Orléans* (The Spire of Orléans), and Soubise de Nogent, known as *Parisien le Soutien du Devoir* (The Parisian Upholder of the *Devoir*). In dealing with a strike by laborers demanding better working conditions, the two architects turned to the Cour des Aides, which gave them full authorization to reorganize the rebellious professional groups. According to some accounts, Soubise and Jacques profited from the occasion to impose on the journeymen new rules inspired by the Catholic faith. Many refused to accept a *devoir* that seemed so different from the one established by Solomon, and the result was a great battle.

> Tools in hand, they became terrible
> And formed two unspeakably enraged camps.
> With blows of the tongs and compass,
> These enemy brothers sowed death.
> Until the end of the day in the city streets
> One heard the sounds of this vile struggle
> Glory to our *devoir!* Long live Liberty!
> In the Loire, at midnight, some were drowned.
> In the gentlest hearts, the notion of the rules
> Incited fury against all adepts
> Of the opposing *devoir;* and the insane fight,
> Which was to divide them for five years,
> Continued all night by lamplight.
> At dawn, on the flat barges known as *gavottes*,
> The few survivors of the Padoréta clan
> Descended the Loire shaking their fists.
> —Raoul Vergez, known as *Béarnais l'Ami du Tour de France*
> (The Friend of the Tour de France from Béarne)

These lines from a poem recycle images traditionally associated with the legendary schism in Orléans. This division of the fellowship of journeymen into two branches, one

AIMONS NOUS
LES UNS LES AUTRES

UNISSONS NOUS
C'EST NOTRE DEVOIR

B

Preceding pages: **Jean-Baptiste Bourguet (1827–1900), known as** *Forézien Bon Desire* **(The Desirable One from Foréze), lithograph representing the three founding fathers of fellowship accompanied by their respective "children"**

Below: **Detail from the colors, or ceremonial garb, of a** *gavot* **dignitary, 1859**

Right: **Postcard of a fellowship contingent from the 1929 Joan-of-Arc Day parade in Orléans**

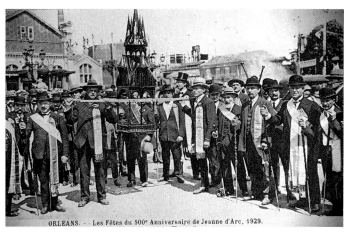

ORLÉANS. — Les Fêtes du 500ᵉ Anniversaire de Jeanne d'Arc, 1929.

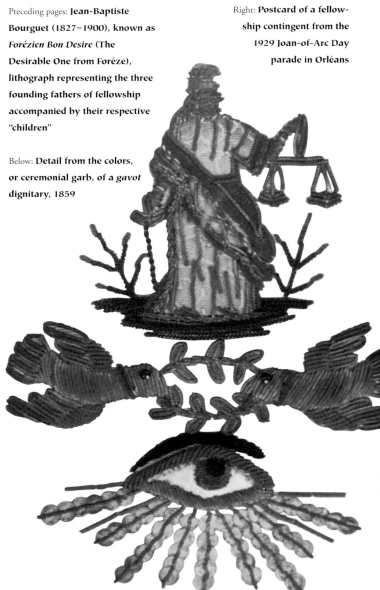

Below: **Detail of an 1850 print. In the second half of the nineteenth century, Masonic influence was very strong in many fellowship chapters.**

Christian and the other based on freedom of conscience, dates from the early fifteenth century. This legend was inspired by an actual event: the split between Catholic and Protestant journeymen. In 1568, Protestants demolished the spire over the transept of Orléans Cathedral, seriously damaging much of the building. This documented incident was incorporated into journeyman legend as the famous schism of the *devoirs*, although, as so often in legends, this version of events is rife with anachronisms.

The Wars of Religion

Through the Orléans myth, it becomes evident that religious quarrels shattered the unity and fraternity of the fellowship. Some maintain that the nickname *étrangers* (foreigners) was occasioned by the Revocation of the Edict of Nantes (1685), which obliged many Protestant journeymen to leave France. Others hold that the *devoir de liberté* began its life as a call for freedom from compulsory confession.

The brawls between rival orders were most intense in the first half of the nineteenth century. Fueled as much by the legends as by religious and political differences, they claimed dozens of victims on the Tour de France. Eventually, journeymen like Agricol Perdiguier denounced the absurdity of

such struggles, which weakened the workers' cause in the eyes of government authorities, who were pleased to see discord prevail among rival orders of journeymen.

During the late nineteenth century many songs were published about this dissension, written by journeymen of every rite following the example of Perdiguier, who was the first to denounce these fratricidal quarrels. Following such evaluation of the laborers' strife, the Tour de France became more peaceful, although occasional brawls proved that tensions between rival fellowships persisted.

The prominent role accorded Jerusalem in fellowship legend indicates the organization's concern in rooting its traditions in the sacred. By tracing its history back to the construction of Solomon's Temple, it provided itself with a lineage whose values were not exclusively historical. Likewise, the tragic episode in Orléans indicates that journeyman organizations were not immune to the passions that have always been factors in uniting or dividing people.

Today, the legends figure much less prominently in the journeymen's educational curriculum. Jerusalem and Orléans no longer trigger heated exchanges among the young journeymen living in a postindustrial society. Rivalries between *devoirs* are not as intense as in the past; nonetheless, each branch of the fellowship cultivates its differences and its specific identity.

Below: **Postcard of a fellowship contingent marching in a Joan-of-Arc Day parade in Orléans, 1908. Note the *devoir* banner in the foreground.**

Bottom: **Print with symbolic journeyman imagery, 1850**

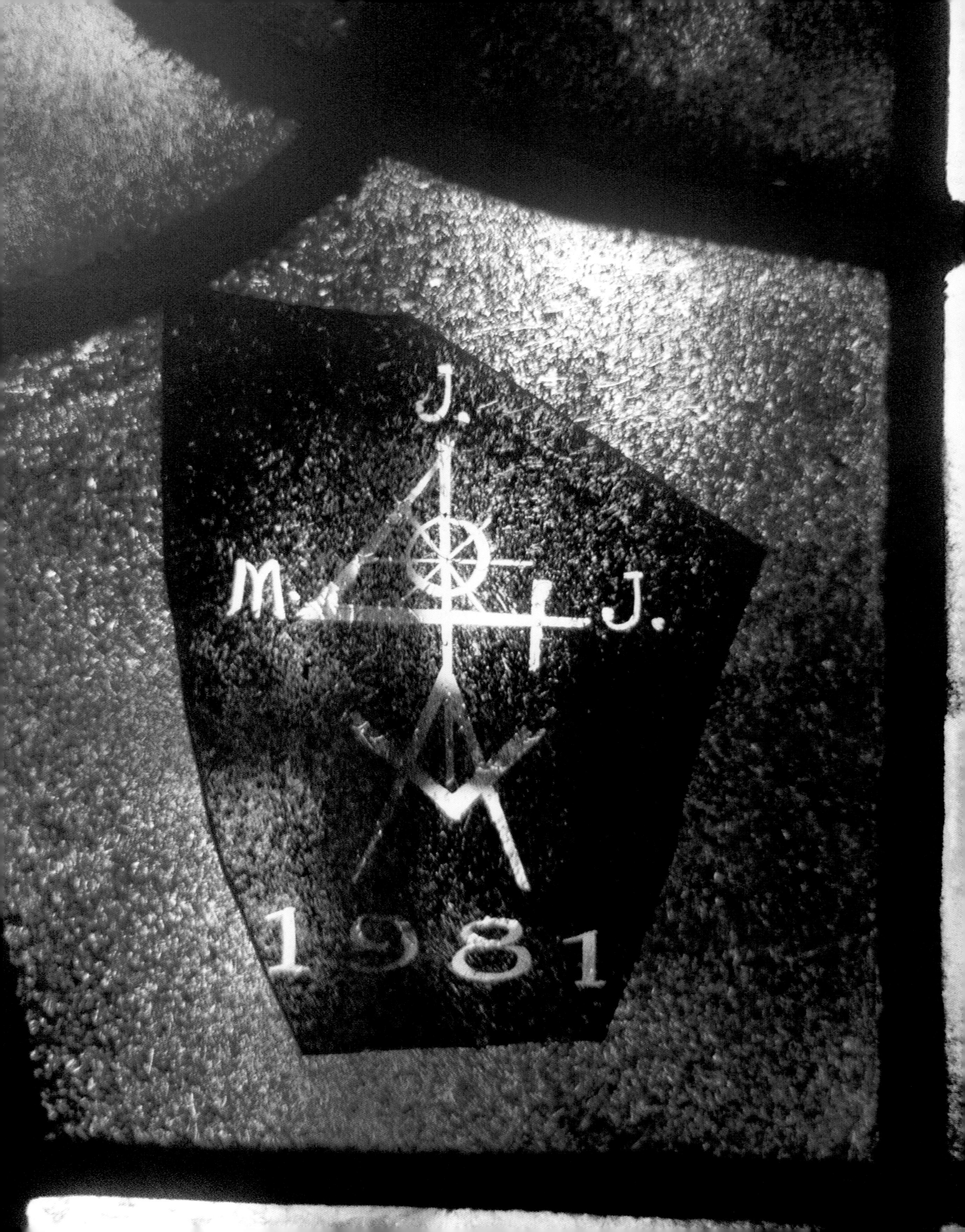
J.
M.
J.
1981

Sainte-Baume, Journeyman Pilgrimage Site

The Pilgrimage of the *Devoir*

Sainte-Baume in Provence is a holy place on the Tour de France of journeymen of the *devoir*. In fellowship legend, it is associated with Master Jacques, who, after seeking refuge there, was assassinated under circumstances reminiscent of the Passion of Christ. By making the pilgrimage to Baume, journeymen of the *devoir* also honored Mary Magdalene, who, after being banished from Palestine, chose to settle in the mountains of Provence near Saint-Maximin, where she led a life of penitence and contemplation for thirty-three years.

Until the end of the nineteenth century, the Tour de France of a journeyman of the *devoir* was considered incomplete until he had made this pilgrimage. Even today, many journeymen imitate their predecessors by gathering in Baume. Is this a mere tourist stop, or a gesture rich in symbolic import? An explanation is provided by *Blois l'Ami du Travail* (The Friend of Work from Blois), a baker journeyman of the *devoir*, in a pamphlet published in 1972 with the title *La Sainte-Baume, haut lieu du compagnonnage* (Sainte-Baume, high place of *compagnonnage*): "We journeymen of the *devoir* have made this pilgrimage as our predecessors did, as will those who follow us, in order to draw from the well of our history the strength necessary to maintain and carry on our spiritual patrimony and continue the mission of the *compagnonnage*."

The Sainte-Baume of Master Jacques

As previously noted, Master Jacques chose to spend his last years in Baume in Provence. His return to Gaul is consistent with a circular narrative often encountered in tales of heroism—after a long voyage of initiation that took him to Jerusalem, Master Jacques returned to his native land. His actions set an example for journeymen of the Tour de France, who likewise traveled far from their homes but returned after completing their tour enriched and transformed by their experiences. It is worth emphasizing the multitude of messages contained in journeyman myths and legends. Even those without training in mythography can

Above: **"Sign of four" carved into the wood of a bench in the grotto at Sainte-Baume**

Below: ***The Union of the Heads of the Bodies of State**, symbolic lithograph by Jean-Baptiste Bourguet, 1870. In the background at left, Sainte-Baume*

make out veiled allusions to fundamental tenets of the journeyman philosophy: the importance of traveling and continuing to learn.

It is in Baume that the traits attributed to Master Jacques most closely resemble those of Christ. Withdrawal, prayer, meditation in the forest, the teaching of disciples who, in turn, will transmit the message, betrayal by one of the faithful who delivers him to his executioners: all these elements of the narrative have analogues in the story of the Passion of Christ. Like Judas, the traitor who sold Jacques to his assassins was overcome by remorse and committed suicide. Incontestably, the shaping and composition of this episode in the legends indicates the Christianization of a fellowship that transformed itself into a *Saint-Devoir de Dieu*, or holy obligation to God. It is worth noting that the *devoir de liberté* always excluded the trip to Sainte-Baume from its tour itinerary, thereby indicating its desire to remain free of all ties to the Catholic Church at a time when religion separated the orders of journeymen.

However important this message, it was not the only one associated with Baume. Any discussion of the symbolism of the site must take into account the figure of Mary Magdalene, whose identification with the place further enriches the notion of spiritual enlightenment associated with it.

The Sainte-Baume of Mary Magdalene

According to legend, the Sanhedrin, alarmed by the rapid spread of Christ's teachings after his death, decided to react vigorously against the adepts of the new religion. Naturally, the first to be targeted were Jesus' friends. Lazarus, Mary Magdalene, Maximin, Martha, Mary Salome (mother of the apostles James the Greater and John the Evangelist), and Mary Cléophas (sister of the Virgin) were taken to the port of Jaffa and put on a boat without sail or rudder. Delivered to the mercy of the waves, the group of exiles reached the shore of Provence, at the mouth of the Rhône River. Soon after disembarking they went their various ways. Mary Salome and Mary Cléophas remained where they were, a site that became known as Saintes-Marie-de-la-Mer. Three others dispersed to Tarascon, Marseilles, and Aix. Mary Magdalene, wishing to pursue a life of solitary contemplation, roamed Provence until she found the grotto in Baume in which she would reside for thirty-three years, some nine hundred years after the arrival and death nearby of Master Jacques.

Mary Magdalene was elevated by journeymen of the *devoir* to the status of patron saint. Given the explicit Christian affiliations of a fellowship calling itself the Saint-Devoir de Dieu, such a gesture is not surprising. But the story of Mary Magdalene's withdrawal to a place that had previously sheltered the founding father of the *devoir* made her an ideal symbolic figure for its journeymen, who elaborated a rich account of spiritual progress around the life of this repentant sinner.

The core of the message associated with Mary Magdalene is contained in Christ's reply upon appearing to her in the guise of a gardener. About to verify his existence by touch,

Right: **Souvenir lithograph of the pilgrimage to Sainte-Baume, 1863**

Below: **Entry inscribed by** *Blois l'Ami du Trait* **(The Friend of the** *Trait* **from Blois), carpenter journeyman of the** *devoir*, **in the travel register after his pilgrimage in 1873. The custom of registering continues.**

Mary Magdalene heard him say: "*Noli me tangere*" ("Do not touch me"). These three words offer many opportunities for interpretation. They recall the famous LDP (*liberté de passer*, "freedom of passage"), the right of member-journeymen to travel from work site to work site with complete freedom. If anyone should try to impede their journey, they could, in effect, proclaim "*Noli me tangere*," for ecclesiastical or lordly authorizations made them untouchable in their capacity as laborers helping to build a castle or a cathedral. Sacred affiliations protected journeymen from secular interference.

Beyond this first reading, we must consider Mary Magdalene in relation to the fellowship's claim to foster progress toward the spiritual. Without spirit, all human works are condemned to disappear; material works perish but the spirit abides. This is one of the principal messages propagated by the rule of the *devoir*, which reminds its newly inducted members: "Now you know how to elevate yourself from the visible to the invisible."

In the western journeyman tradition, Mary Magdalene represents, through her decision to withdraw from the world at Sainte-Baume, the desire to elevate oneself from the physical to the spiritual. Through this act, she attained true symbolic status, representing to the journeymen of the *devoir*, "visible and material things that facilitate access to the invisible." In addition, journeymen were moved by a Mary Magdalene who each day ritually enacted the story of death (by remaining in the grotto) and resurrection (angels regularly transported her to the summit of Saint-Pilon, the mountain overlooking the grotto, to hear celestial music).

Sainte-Baume as a Pilgrimage Site

Even today, the pilgrimage to Baume figures in the tour itinerary of members of the *devoir*. As in the past, a mark is applied to the colors (ceremonial ribbons and garb) of all journeymen who can prove they have visited the grotto at Saint-Pilon. Every order possesses its own stamp for the purpose. In the nineteenth century, Father Audebaud, who operated a stall at Saint-Maximin, sold special liveries and lithographs to journeymen wishing to have souvenirs of their visits. When attached to branches gathered in the woods around the path leading to the grotto, these souvenirs were known as *pacotilles*.

A visitor to this holy place of *compagnonnage* lacking a journeyman's staff will need a walking stick for the ascent. The stone of several oratories punctuating the path bear journey-

men's marks recalling the nature and orientation of the pilgrimage: it is a path taken by countless journeymen completing their Tour de France. At the end of the forest path, a steep stairway leads to an esplanade on which three bronze crosses recall the meaning of this Christian pilgrimage. After reaching the heart of the grotto, the visitor can admire superb stained-glass windows made by Pierre Petit, known as *Tourangeau le Disciple de la Lumière* (The Disciple of Light from Touraine), journeyman glazier of the Devoirs Unis. These windows alone justify the pilgrimage. A stop before the sarcophagus that supposedly contain relics of Mary Magdalene, then a visit to Saint-Pilon, will conclude a trip to Baume.

The Sainte-Baume of *Pierre le Saintonge*

The following song lyric was written in 1948 by Pierre Morin, journeyman joiner of the *devoir*, known to his brothers by the symbolic name *Pierre le Saintonge* (Pierre from Saintonge):

We are in Provence, everywhere the earth
Awakens the night, which disappears in the distance . . .
The sun illuminates the rocks,
Makes everything new in the pure morning air.
Suddenly, emerging from the shadows,
A white enclosure appears
Above a dark forest,
In these rocks that guard our secrets.

Chorus:
Oh! Sainte-Baume!
Let us sing! We lift our hearts!
Here is the realm of perfect happiness.

Even while following far from the mountains
Our path, which leads to the cool shade
There, in the peace of these ancient vaults,
We ascend to the sacred Calvary.
A stone oratory remains
Where our marks brave the weather
And below the moss a sweet murmur:
Water singing as it drips from the rock.

Marching still, in search of adventure
Among the rocks, which are no longer covered
High above, where, braving nature,
The Saint-Pilon keeps watch over this desert.
Here is shelter, it's the chapel of
Saint Maximin with its gables . . .
Everywhere, we hear your distant call,
Holy place so dear to noble journeymen.

Then, on returning from this holy pilgrimage,
At a gathering of free journeymen,
On our colors, in homage to Baume,
We will receive the seal of the *devoirants*,
In this grotto where Magdalene
Long sought pardon
Where kings and the powerful . . . even queens!
Came to pray, like journeymen.

In my country, far from the song of the cicadas,
Far from Baume and Saint-Maximin,
Tomorrow I will sing, oh city without rival,
in Saintonge close to the sea . . .
All is sun and hope in
Sainte-Baume, and in my heart
I will sing, beautiful Provence,
The gentle secret of your enchanting sites.

LE GÉNIE DU COMPAGNONNAGE FAISANT LE TOUR DU GLOBE.

Par le travail.
le zele.

la prudence
et la conduite

THE HISTORY OF THE *DEVOIRS*

aking their official appearance in the later Middle Ages, the first journeyman confraternities were relatively clandestine organizations. Defying first the guilds ruled by royalty, then the French church, they had no difficulty attracting young men eager for professional and social advancement.

Having survived wars, severe restrictions, and revolution (industrial as well as political), the fellowship of journeymen is now calmly preparing to face the twenty-first century, evidence of its extraordinary ability to adapt to changing circumstances.

Cy coumenteur les chappites du
liure de politique que frere Gilles
augustin euuoya a philippes roy de
france. Du couuencut des roys des priues
Le premier cappitre enseigne
que len doit parler et deuommer
Des choses dout la vie humaine se
puelt estre souftenue il veult donuer
rouguoissance et wot de prouuier
Sa maison et son hostel et sa hen

Le seco̅d cappitre enseigne q̅
les roys et les priuces doiuet faire
ttauc edifieme̅t et subtilleme̅t
fais et en lou air et en sain et en

Lieu houneste
Le tiers cappitre enseigne en
quel lieu et en quelles parties de la
terre les roys et les priuces doiuent
edifier leurs mesnages et leurs arcs
Le quart cappitre enseigne q̅
nature enclme lou̅e a auoir prestee
Dout il puelt viure en cest siecle
Le quint chappitre enseigne q̅
ce est graut proffit a la vie humaine
que chm̅ homs ait ses ppres richesses
et ses propres pressious terriennes
Le sixte cappitre escuigne ame̅t
len doit vser des biens temporelz et

Seven Centuries of History

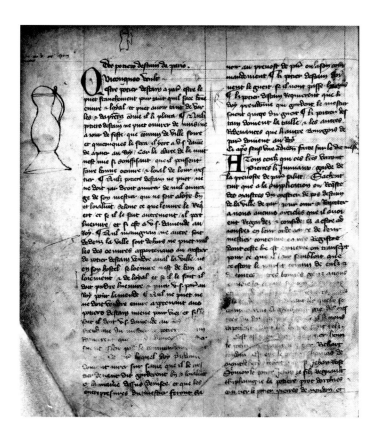

Above: **Page from Étienne Boileau,**
***Livre des métiers* (Book of crafts),**
1268

Opposite: **Fourteenth-century**
miniature, Bibliothèque Sainte-
Geneviève, Paris. Relations
between patrons and contractors
were based on trust. This artist
accurately represented them on
an equal footing.

istorians date the origins of the first organizations that bear any resemblance to the fellowship of journeymen to the period of the Crusades and of construction of the great Gothic cathedrals. A simple reading of the hierarchical lists of crafts, so numerous in the nineteenth century, confirms this, for the crafts involved in construction of the cathedrals are given priority. Wood, stone, and iron were the founding triad of the first groups of laborers to organize themselves into a *devoir*.

Scholars who study the history of *compagnonnage* have few tools with which to work. Fellowship archives contain little information that predates the eighteenth century. The organization always emphasized oral tradition, which means that events important in its history were not always recorded and transmitted in writing. Researchers will have better luck with the edicts, ordinances, and other decrees of the realm and its parlements, which are rich in information pertaining to the Tour de France. Precious data can also be gleaned from police records, monitories, and other ecclesiastical judgments for certain periods.

The *Livre des Métiers*

Drafted in 1268, after many years of data collection and hearings overseen by the Provost of Paris, Étienne Boileau, the *Livre des métiers* (Book of crafts) is an indispensable document for anyone studying the practices, customs, and traditions of the medieval guilds. It was commissioned by Louis IX, who, concerned about the existence of unbridled professional bodies, resolved to establish a set of regulations so as to minimize disturbances. One of its many rules is of particular interest here, for it is an early reference to itinerant workers: "It is henceforth forbidden for any worker to leave his master without his approval."

Before proceeding further with our discussion of the medieval guilds, we should clarify the relevant terminology, since it can generate confusion. Under the Old Regime, crafts were organized around three professional *états*, or status levels: apprentice, journeyman (*compagnon*), and master. It is important to understand the difference between guild journeymen and journeymen of the Tour de France. The former was a worker who, throughout his life, remained in the service of the same master, and never obtained the status of mas-

Right: **Fifteenth-century miniature, Vienna. Square rules, like the one presented here by a patron to a contractor, symbolized the solid and right-angled nature of stone blocks, and, by association, all the work at the site.**

Below: **Since the Middle Ages, travel has been the very essence of the journeyman's life.**

ter with his own workshop; the latter was a journeyman seeking to affirm his independence in the face of the conservatism of the guilds that offered him no hope of improving his lot, unless he was the son or son-in-law of a master, which provided the only possibility of obtaining the coveted mastership. This longing to travel and desire for liberty in the work marketplace was in profound contradiction with the rules laid down in the *Livre des métiers.* Faced with the near impossibility of blossoming within the corporative cell, discontented workers founded clandestine organizations to assure their survival. When the guilds became a dead end, the journeymen established their own group. This group gradually became a strong and true fraternal community, and spread throughout France.

As the word *"compagnonnage"* has been coined relatively recently, in the nineteenth century, it is best to use the term *"devoir"* when referring to these early workers' associations.

Historical Emergence

1420: King Charles VI drafted an ordinance concerning the cobblers of the city of Troyes in which an allusion to the journeyman of the Tour de France is clearly made: "Several journeymen and workers of the said craft, of various languages and nations, came and went from town to town to work, learn, experience, see, and know one another."

1480: A painting entitled *The Siege of Rhodes* by Guglielmo Caourcino represents the ritual induction of journeyman carpenters and stonecutters by the hospitalers of Saint-Jean de Jérusalem.

1506: During the reign of Louis XII, a sentence handed down by the Châtelet contains a detailed account of an organization that seems to have been highly structured: "Having made and upheld prohibition against those declaring themselves king and journeymen of the craft of couturier, they have no more power and authority than the other varlets and apprentices of the said craft to make any assemblies, companies, conventicles, confraternities, dinners, suppers, or banquets to deal with their affairs, on pain of imprisonment." As kings succeeded one another, prohibitions proliferated, proof of the resistance of a *devoir* that apparently was attracting more and more young men. Archival sources indicate the existence of societies resembling journeymen fellowships in many cities, including Paris, Lyon, Toulouse, Dijon, and Reims. The *devoir* was being organized everywhere to receive itinerant workers on the Tour de France.

1539: In the ordinance of Villers-Cotterêts, François I reiterated the prohibitions of his predecessors: "In accordance with our old ordinances and with the decisions of our sovereign courts, all craft and artisanal fraternities will be destroyed, forbidden, and prohibited throughout our realm."

1540: A report in the judicial archives of Dijon cites journeymen names such as Robert de Pontoyse and Jehan de la Mothe. These two journeyman cobblers "went to eat at the house of a woman called the *mère* [mother]." Furthermore, Jehan de la Mothe, a native of Tours, told his interrogator he had been traveling for four years and had visited the cities of Blaye-sur-Loire, Saumur, Angers, Nantes, Fontenay, Bordeaux, Poitiers, Nevers, Courbay, Villeneuve-le-Roi, Avallon, and Dijon. Thus by the mid-sixteenth century the Tour de France was a structured reality: the existence of "mothers," as the women who ran the chapter houses were called, allows no room for doubt.

1571: During the reign of Charles IX, an edict reveals various aspects of the *devoir* to us, for it condemns all manner of confraternities, oaths, monopolies, dues, captains, banners, gathering places, banquets, festivals, assemblies, and staffs.

The Religious Problem

Until the early seventeenth century, chapters of the *devoir* proliferated, focusing on the reception of itinerant workers and offering job placement, shelter, solidarity, and mutual aid. Hitherto, the monarchy had been the only adversary of the journeymen, who, by braving the guilds, were daring to defy royal authority. Despite repeated regulations and restrictions, the *devoir* continued to prosper.

The seventeenth century marked an important turning point in the history of *compagnonnage*, for the Church of France also began to condemn it. The Catholic faith could no longer tolerate workers' associations that had appropriated elements of Christian symbolism for use in its induction rituals. In addition to the legends intimating parallels between the lives of Master Jacques and Christ, the *devoir* "baptized" its "children," going so far as to use the Bible during the swearing of the obligatory oaths of fidelity.

Between 1645 and 1648, the religious confraternity of the Très-Saint-Sacrement-de-l'Autel (Very Holy Sacrament of the Altar) set out to expose the induction ceremonies used by journeyman saddlers and cobblers of the *devoir*, denouncing their practices as intolerable attacks against the faith. The result of these monitories was the decision of the doctors of the faculty of Paris, published March 14, 1655, denouncing "the impious,

Above: **Oath of journeyman saddlers of the *devoir*, Bordeaux, 1654. Fraught relations between the journeyman chapters and the Church were caused by the oaths and rituals used in induction ceremonies.**

Below: **The makers of *sabots* (wooden clogs), who initially lived in groups on the outskirts of villages, were allied with the journeyman cleavers and charcoal sellers.**

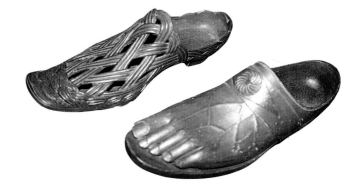

Fifteenth-century miniature, Library of Vienna. Every laborer was assigned a well-defined role in accordance with his level of craft expertise in the hierarchical guild of construction workers.

sacrilegious, and superstitious practices current in several crafts of the *devoir*."

In concert with the official act of condemnation, the Church of France attempted to instigate a counterorganization within the confraternities in the guise of a brotherhood of cobblers, a semi-religious order overseen by Henri Buch. After Buch's death in 1666 the new organization fell apart, rendering the strategy a total failure. Accustomed to operating undercover, the *devoir* was organized so that no impediments, whether royal or religious in origin, could hinder its expansion among a laboring population searching for structure outside of the guild system. Fraternal and efficient, the journeyman organizations seemed destined for a bright future. But internal tensions soon created new problems.

The revocation of the Edict of Nantes in 1685 had grave consequences for the world of journeymen seeking unity. Catholic and Protestant "brothers" could no longer live within a single "family." The powerful Saint-Devoir de Dieu, an umbrella organization overseeing all Catholic journeymen, was countered by another association that brought together

Below and opposite: **Pages from the weekly illustrated magazine *L'Illustration*, 1845. Religious and political differences, along with the determination to safeguard hiring monopolies, were the main causes of brawls between rival journeyman groups.**

journeymen declaring themselves to be "*non du devoir*" (not of the *devoir*). Increasingly, the Catholic Church ignored its condemnation of 1655 and took the journeyman movement under its tutelage and benevolent oversight, maintaining that the organization need only revise its rituals. A telling indication of this new policy dates from 1758, when the Carmelite convent in the city of Nantes opened its doors to the local chapter of journeyman joiners of the *devoir*. By contrast, Protestants and nonbelievers formed their own *devoir*, which later, during the French Revolution, took the name *devoir de liberté* ("duty" or "rite" of liberty).

Despite this historical split, which occasioned the legends of Orléans, the *devoirs* did not lose sight of their original mission and vocation. Many sources in French provincial archives attest to the journeymen's solidarity in the face of the officially sanctioned power of the guilds. As a way of resisting the guild masters, journeymen devised an effective system of defense and demand. Strikes and *interdits de boutique*—bans on working for intransigent masters—became formidable weapons. Although weakened by their difficulties with church authorities, journeyman confraternities would, paradoxically, come to occupy a unique role as defender of the world of labor.

"There is a spirit of rebellion so deeply rooted that in commercial cities one sees between 700 and 800 workers in a single factory refuse to come to work because their daily salary is to be reduced by one sou. . . . They even have their own statutes, some of which are written down and passed from hand to hand. . . . It is declared that if any one of them should agree to work for less than the standard rate, he is to be banished immediately from the craft." Such was the view of *compagnonnage* as seen by the master tailors in the city of Lyon in 1688.

A Militant and Divided *Compagnonnage*

From the first decades of the eighteenth century, *compagnonnage* was characterized by two aspects. The many manuscript and printed sources dating from this period leave no doubt as to the vigilance of journeyman organizations regarding working conditions and hiring practices, making it clear that they were always willing to organize strikes, sometimes over extended periods, to obtain satisfaction from recalcitrant masters. On the other hand, these same documents indicate that the journeyman network was increasingly beset by tensions between rival rites. The resulting differences sometimes erupted into violent disputes between enemy *devoirs*.

An often-cited ordinance issued by the governor of Montpellier in 1730 is an important document in the history of the journeyman organizations. Here, for the first time, the word "syndicate" is used to describe such groups, offering further evidence of their initial vocation: "What provokes them still

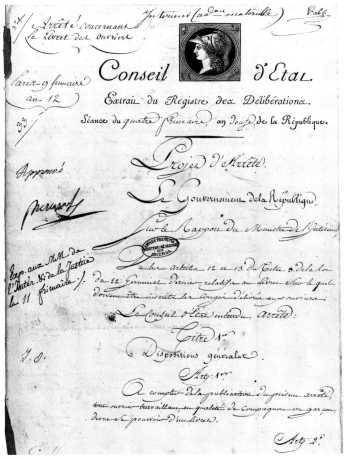

man organizations successfully instituted hiring monopolies in many cities, becoming increasingly intransigent in their relations with guild masters. When a master refused to accede to their demands, the journeymen organized a boycott of his shop, obliging him to reconsider under threat of bankruptcy. And when masters joined forces to confront the journeymen, the latter placed the entire city under strike, or *interdit*, preventing all nonjourneyman workers from coming to the aid of the guilds.

Powerful and determined to prevail, the journeymen could have become a serious danger to social order. Struggles between rival rites effectively defused this threat.

Disappointed Hopes of the Revolution

With the edicts of Turgot, issued in 1776, the guilds knew their end was near. The French Revolution of 1789 only completed a process that had been under way since the final years of the Old Regime. After the dissolution of the guilds, journeyman associations were the only entities capable of organizing the labor market.

The 1791 passage of the Allarde law promised to transform a centuries-old dream of *compagnonnage* into reality: "Beginning on April 1, all citizens will be free to exercise any profession or craft they like, after having obtained a license and paid the necessary fee." But two months later, the Le Chapelier law upset optimistic expectations by prohibiting workers' associations, including those of *compagnonnage*. At the height of the

more to disorder is that, by punishable abuse, they have undertaken to create syndicates amongst themselves . . . so we have those in one syndicate against those in another, and all of them together against the masters."

The example of Montpellier should not obscure the multitude of documents attesting to brawls between rival societies. In 1745, the Parlement of Angers sentenced several journeyman carpenters of the *devoir* "to be attached to the yoke of the pillory in the said town, on a market day, with signs placed before and behind them bearing the words 'journeymen of the *devoir*' and 'disturbers of the public peace.'" The guild masters, however, did not admit defeat. They filed legal complaints just about everywhere, but in most cases these remained without effect. Thus, in 1779, an ordinance issued by the police in Blois repeated that "it is henceforth forbidden for journeymen to assemble, to leave masters, and to accept jobs on their own." Some cities tried establishing employment offices, threatening to expel all newly arrived workers who found positions through means other than this municipal service. Despite such measures, journey-

Above: **The institution of the *livret d'ouvrier* (workers' registration book) was intended to improve control of the movements and activities of itinerant workers on the Tour de France.**

violence during the Revolution, the various journeyman organizations were obliged to keep a low profile, covertly continuing their educational activities and generosity toward a world of labor caught in the whirlwind of political and social events.

This same revolutionary period saw the official birth of the *devoir de liberté*. The first chapter of journeyman carpenters of the *devoir de liberté* was established in Paris on May 5, 1804. All journeymen not affiliated with the Saint-Devoir-de-Dieu joined the new organization, which was placed under the symbolic patronage of King Solomon. Henceforth, the various groups of journeymen "not of the *devoir*" were known as *loups* (wolves), *étrangers* (foreigners), *indiens* (indians), and *gavots* (montagnards), all under the collective umbrella of the *devoir de liberté*. Protestants, atheists, and freethinkers immediately joined ranks with this new family. Chapters were soon established in Tours, Dijon, Auxerre, Nîmes, Lyon, Marseilles, Toulouse, Montpellier, and Bordeaux.

Under Napoleon, the *livret d'ouvrier*, or workers' registration booklet, assumed its full importance. An efficient means of control, this booklet, which all journeymen were obliged to carry and keep up to date, made it possible for the authorities to better track journeymen's movements. Articles 415 and 416 of this little document are revealing: "All coalitions among workers in view of simultaneous work stoppages will be pun-

ished by two to five years in prison." And later, "Workers will also be punished who have pronounced penalties, prohibitions, interdictions, or condemnations." These lines clearly target journeymen's associations.

Toward Unification of the *Devoirs*

In the first half of the nineteenth century, *compagnonnage* reached its apogee. Membership in the *devoir* and the *devoir de liberté* during this period has been estimated from 200,000 to 500,000. The organizations were the defenders of workers' demands and offered protective and efficient structure. But animosity between rival societies occasioned numerous police reports and received high-profile coverage in the press. In 1839, a young journeyman joiner belonging to the *devoir de liberté* published a *Livre du compagnonnage* (Book of journeyman organizations). In this book, the author introduced *compagnonnage* to a larger public, suggesting that dissension might cease if the *devoirs* were unified. Such was the beginning of a long and difficult task. Agricol Perdiguier, known as *Avignonnait la Vertu* (The Virtuous One from Avignon), devoted his entire life to it.

From the middle of the nineteenth century, *compagnonnage* was undermined from within. In some quarters, the process of renewal undertaken by Perdiguier was resisted. The religious disputes of earlier days had given way to political disagreement. Reactions to the Revolution of 1848, for example, were various. Under Perdiguier's impetus, there was a short-lived reconciliation and unification of the various rites. Several journeymen dared to run for the National Assembly. Perdiguier and a few others were elected, but they later paid dearly for this action by being exiled after the coup d'état of the future Napoleon III.

Decline

Under the Second Empire of France, mechanization and capitalism accelerated, fostering specialized tasking in large factories. A new world was taking shape. The universal expositions of 1855 and 1867 made the public aware of the great changes being wrought by machines. The ancestral professional foundations of *compagnonnage* were seriously threatened by these

Above and right: **The railroad was a major symbol of the early Industrial Revolution. The Tour de France on foot—with its associated rituals and folklore—and manual skills that had been refined over centuries were threatened by mechanization and increasing capitalism, which nearly killed the institution.**

Opposite, top: **Jean Bernard (1908–1994) on the right, founder of the Association Ouvrière des Compagnons du Devoir. His charisma, coupled with the variety of his interests and achievements (he was a painter, sculptor, philosopher), made him a key figure in contemporary French *compagnonnage*.**

developments, which devalued the craft secrets and manual skills so dear to journeymen. Within a few years, young workers turned away from the fellowship, which they judged severely because of its internal strife. Although the journeymen tried to regroup, ingrained conservatism prevented all such attempts.

After the tragic Commune of Paris in 1871, in which Parisian workers rebelled against the government and were brutally repressed, *compagnonnage* was further weakened and disoriented. In 1875, Perdiguier died, having never realized his initial project. However, beginning in 1884, workers' syndicates could be formed without government authorization. This was a great milestone in the history of *compagnonnage*. In 1889, at the instigation of the journeyman Lucien Blanc, known as *Provençal le Résolu* (The Resolute One from Provence), the Union Compagnonnique des Compagnons du Tour de France des Devoirs Unis was founded. But this movement was unable to unify all of the *devoirs*, as it was considered too innovative by journeymen attached to a certain traditional idea of *compagnonnage*. They countered by trying to organize journeymen "*restés fidèles au devoir*" (still faithful to the *devoir*).

By the end of the nineteenth century, *compagnonnage* had lost its grandeur as well as its power. Mechanization had definitively conquered the world of large-scale industry, and now threatened the realm of small-scale industry; the very notion of apprenticeship of young men was undermined by the rampant hiring of unskilled workers and children. The rapid spread of railroads greatly disoriented *compagnonnage* by rendering obsolete the Tour de France on foot. Furthermore, the advent of electricity changed the tools used in many professions, making traditional skills irrelevant. Confronted by this new world of labor, syndicates responded to the expectations of new generations as best they could. By using an ingenious propaganda campaign, the first syndicates made a mockery of journeyman customs. A new page was being turned.

Toward Renewal

In 1901, Étienne Martin Saint-Léon published his book *Le Compagnonnage*, in which he predicted that the venerable institution would soon vanish. World War I brought heavy losses to all journeyman organizations, and at the end of the conflict the state of *compagnonnage* was worse than precarious. Nonetheless, some journeymen tried to envision a new form of *compagnonnage* better adapted to modern society, although relations between the young Union Compagnonnique and the old *devoirs* were less than cordial, impeding unification of the rites.

World War II brought about a profound change in the world of *compagnonnage*. In 1941, at the height of France's occupation, a renewal campaign was organized by a group of journeymen of the *devoir* led by a young stonecutter, Jean Bernard, known as *La Fidelité d'Argenteuil* (The Faithful One from Argenteuil). With the protection and support of Marshal Pétain, he visited several cities on the Tour de France to explain his plan and obtain the consent of various journeyman associations. After countless preparatory meetings, Marshal Pétain granted a charter of *compagnonnage*, delivered at Commentry on May 1, 1941. Thus was born the Association Ouvrière des Compagnons du Devoir du Tour de France.

This attempt to rejuvenate *compagnonnage* did not succeed in unifying all of the organizations, some preferring to wait for the country's liberation before joining the experimental group. After the war, the Union Compagnonnique, which had been dormant during the occupation, resumed its activities. In November of 1945, the two rites of carpenters merged: the *indiens* and the *soubises* joined forces to create a consolidated organization of journeyman carpenters of the *devoir*. After a referendum and much controversy, this organization refused to affiliate itself with the Association Ouvrière. In the early 1950s, it became the keystone of a new *compagnonnage*, the Fédération Compagnonnique des Métiers du Bâtiment.

The history of *compagnonnage* in France does not end with the years following the country's liberation. Since then, many events have enriched the great book of the *devoirs*. In 1953, an umbrella entity consolidating all the European journeyman organizations was established, the Confédération des Compagnonnages Européens. Every five years, it sponsors a large conference bringing together journeymen from across Europe to meet and discuss common goals. Thanks to this pan-European confederation, young workers can now travel throughout Europe, benefiting from a system of reception and placement.

At the dawn of the twenty-first century, the various journeyman families report, with satisfaction, that their memberships are growing. New chapters are being established, proof of the continuing dynamism and vitality of *compagnonnage*. Far from wallowing in nostalgia, today's journeymen are involved in every construction project requiring highly skilled labor. At the end of the nineteenth century, journeyman carpenters of the *devoir de liberté* set out for America to oversee exceptional building projects, and they are still in demand abroad, for the quality of their work is known throughout the world. Without a doubt, many pages in the history of *compagnonnage* have yet to be written.

COMPAGNONNAGE TODAY

s in the past, modern-day *compagnonnage* is a multifaceted organization. The Union Compagnonnique des Devoirs Unis, founded in 1889, continues its policy of openness to many crafts. The Association Ouvrière des Compagnons du Devoir has evolved considerably since the 1940s, when it came into existence. The Fédération Compagnonnique des Métiers du Bâtiment, established in the 1950s, completes the landscape of French *compagnonnage*, whose membership is growing steadily after a long period of stagnation.

A Diverse *Compagnonnage*

Above: **National headquarters of the Union Compagnonnique, Versailles**

Opposite: **The Union Compagnonnique has welcomed many crafts long excluded from journeyman organizations, for example, chefs and cooks.**

From the beginning, *compagnonnage* has constantly evolved, changing with its many component organizations. It is therefore worth clarifying a point of vocabulary that might otherwise be a source of confusion. Like "*devoir*," the word "*compagnonnage*" is used to designate the entire institution in all its diversity, even as it figures in the names of the various journeyman families. Since the end of World War II, French *compagnonnage* has consisted of three organizations, each of which has its own history, its own trajectory, its particular identity. Despite some important differences between them, all three families are descendants of the old journeyman societies, which in turn had very different notions about what it meant to be a professed journeyman.

Since the early days, rivalries growing out of religious and political disagreements have faded into the background. Today, one's organizational affiliation is almost a matter of chance: a relative, a friend, even an advertisement can prompt a young person, who perhaps sees in modern *compagnonnage* a path that will lead to fulfillment of his or her aspirations as a craftsperson or an artist. For example, a youngster who wants to become a journeyman cook must become affiliated with the Union Compagnonnique des Devoirs Unis, the only one of the three organizations to acknowledge and accept this craft. In a Europe constantly engaged in creative enterprises, French *compagnonnage* has a special role to play. It is the guardian and guarantor of the workers' body of knowledge, their ethic, and tradition.

The Union Compagnonnique des Compagnons du Tour de France des Devoirs Unis

This is the oldest of the three extant French journeyman organizations. It was officially created on September 5, 1889, at an important gathering in Paris of several journeyman associations that had previously formed a federation. Bringing together journeymen from all three rites (Solomon, Jacques, and Soubise), this movement was conceived in the spirit of Perdiguier's unification plan.

By pursuing this strategy of unification, the Union Compagnonnique sought to bring together the maximum number of journeymen seeking structure at a moment when the nascent syndicates were proving attractive to new generations of workers. This was the principal mission of the first president and founder of the Union Compagnonnique, Lucien Blanc, journeyman harness maker of the *devoir*. At his instigation, the young Union solicited many recruits from the scattered journeyman associations. In 1909, the Union boasted three thousand members in forty chapters along the Tour de France. But the enthusiasm of the first years was short-lived. More and more journeymen of the *devoir* and the *devoir de liberté* (commonly referred to as the old *devoirs*) began to reproach the Union for its disregard of centuries-old traditions. Some denounced the high rate of induction, claiming it entailed a sacrifice of quality for quantity. Old quarrels about the acceptance of crafts hitherto remote from the traditions of *compagnonnage* resurfaced. The idea of accepting all crafts indiscriminately, without prioritizing one over another, was the crucial point of divergence between the old *devoirs* and the young Union Compagnonnique. Finally, many compagnons of the *devoir*, who were fervent Catholics, denounced a certain Masonic influence that, according to them, manifested itself in the rituals used in the chapters. Furthermore, Lucien Blanc's membership in a Masonic temple was exploited to the full by his detractors.

The death of Blanc in 1909 and the death tolls of World War I shortly afterward were serious blows to the spread of the Union Compagnonnique. Rather than join an organization they judged too innovative, many journeymen preferred to remain isolated, no longer believing that their ideal of journeyman fellowship had a future. World War II only intensified the crisis of a French *compagnonnage* in search of its vocation.

With the creation of the Association Ouvrière des Compagnons du Devoir in 1941, the Union Compagnonnique saw a new attempt to renew the traditions of *compagnonnage*, fifty-two years after the launching of its own ill-fated effort. Although it followed the first steps of this initiative with interest, the Union increasingly distanced itself from the new movement, which it considered too closely tied to the Vichy regime. Thus after the liberation, the Union Compagnonnique resumed its activities and reasserted its independence from the Association Ouvrière des Compagnons du Devoir.

Since then, the Union Compagnonnique des Devoirs Unis has cultivated several distinct features. It remains the only journeyman fellowship to use the same induction ritual for all

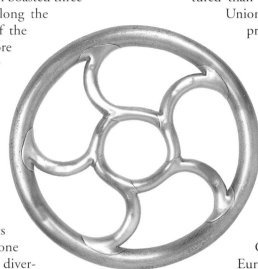

The iron crafts have traditionally been associated with French *compagnonnage*.

crafts. Having brought about a unification of the *devoirs*, its rite is called trinitarian because it incorporates elements of the rites of Solomon, Jacques, and Soubise. Divided into sections, the Union Compagnonnique accepts many more professions than the two other organizations combined. *Santonniers* (makers of crèche figurines), *chocolatiers*, jewelers, chefs, and cooks are among the craft practitioners who make up its unique profile. Although its Tour de France is much less structured than the two other journeyman families, the Union offers quality training that can result in a professional license or a certificate of *maîtrise*. Administratively, each section regularly elects a board under the authority of a president of the section house. All of the sections that constitute the Tour de France report to a board of general directors headed by a *président général*, the official spokesperson for the Union Compagnonnique des Devoirs Unis. A national congress is held every three years.

Although the Union left the Confédération des Compagnonnage Européens in 1988, it was, with the Fédération Compagnonnique des Métiers du Bâtiment, one of the prime engines behind the establishment of this pan-European confederation of journeymen organizations.

The Association Ouvrière des Compagnons du Devoir du Tour de France

The movement toward unification was founded thanks to the efforts of a young journeyman stonecutter, Jean Bernard, who, at the height of the occupation during World War II, undertook to create an organization that would unite all the various French journeyman fellowships. The result was the Association Ouvrière des Compagnons du Devoir du Tour de France. Through the intervention of Dr. Ménétrel, Jean Bernard was introduced to Marshal Pétain. Bernard then proceeded to make a case for a renewal of the journeyman fellowships, insisting on the corporate character of the association he had in mind, which would in no way resemble a secret society such as Freemasonry. By the end of this meeting, Jean Bernard had won the marshal's confidence: "Journeymen of the Tour de France, one of your own came to see me; he explained things to me, and I grasped the profundity of your institutions." Buttressed by the support of the head of state, from October

Opposite: **In 1987, restoration of the statue of the archangel on Mont-Saint-Michel was entrusted to journeymen of the *devoir* in the workshop of the Fondation de Coubertin. The restored statue was lifted to its lofty perch by helicopter.**

1940 to February 1941, Jean Bernard participated in official and informal meetings in some twenty cities of the Tour de France, presenting his plan for renewing the network of fellowships. For several months after this campaign, the cities of Lyon and Vichy received journeymen-delegates representing various crafts to consider the statutes and functioning of the new organization.

On May 1, 1941, in Commentry, before some three hundred journeymen, Marshal Pétain solemnly issued the charter of the new *compagnonnage* to Jean Bernard, thereby officially creating the Association Ouvrière: "I grant the journeymen of the Tour de France this charter of *compagnonnage*, so as to permit them to revive the traditional and centuries-old virtues of a knighthood of workers issuing from the people, and I charge them to bring its activities to the workers of a resurgent France."

After the opening of its first chapter house in Lyon, the Association advocated a certain idea of *compagnonnage* during a difficult and complex period. Jean Bernard and his circle believed their activities had in no way entailed collaboration with the occupying forces. However, others felt differently, and this movement was not to achieve its goal of integrating the various component organizations of French *compagnonnage*. The Union Compagnonnique resumed its activities, which had been suspended during the war. As for the new body of journeyman carpenters of the *devoir* (formed by a merger in 1945), it refused, after many attempts, to merge with the Association Ouvrière des Compagnons du Devoir du Tour de France. The creation of a third organization seemed imminent, for the Fédération Compagnonnique des Métiers du Bâtiment was in the process of being formed.

The Association Ouvrière did manage to unite the vast majority of chapters professing the rite of Master Jacques. While unable to attract those professing the rite of Solomon, it did bring in a few committed to the rite of Soubise, thanks to a group of journeyman carpenters of the *devoir* who refused to accept the merger of *indiens* and *soubises* negotiated in Paris in November of 1945.

Since 1941, the Association Ouvrière has forged an impressive network of houses of journeymen of the *devoir* throughout France. There are also chapters in Germany, Switzerland, Belgium, Holland, and Canada. A Council of *Compagnonnage* directs the movement and gathers every year at the national headquarters to set the organization's agenda. The first councillor, elected by his peers, is the group's official representative.

Participating in major projects in France, such as the Musée d'Orsay and the Louvre, and throughout the world, for example, the restoration of the Statue of Liberty in New York and the subway in Caracas, Venezuela, journeymen of the *devoir* are also open to recent technological advances. Offering a course of training that culminates in a BTS (a *Brevet de technicien supérieur* degree), the Association Ouvrière is, by far, the most structured of the three journeyman organizations. The crafts accepted by this *compagnonnage* are divided into four subgroups: building crafts, metal crafts, leather and plastic crafts, and crafts relating to food preparation.

The Fédération Compagnonnique des Métiers du Bâtiment

The origins of the third and last of the current journeyman organizations can be traced to the merger of the journeyman carpenters of the *devoir*, *bons drilles* (good fellows) of Father Soubise (also known as *chiens*, or dogs), and the journeyman carpenters of the *devoir de liberté*, children of King Solomon (the *indiens*, sometimes called *loups*, or wolves). On November 25, 1945, in Paris, these long-standing rivals united to form a single group whose members are now known, logically enough, as *chiens-loups* (dog-wolves), carpenter journeymen of the *devoirs* of the Tour de France.

In 1947, after protracted negotiations, this consolidated organization of journeyman carpenters held a referendum on the question of its possible affiliation with the Association Ouvrière des Compagnons du Devoir du Tour de France. The majority of participating chapter houses objected to such an alliance. In 1953, after regrouping around the Vergez, Pelluchon, Breton, and Liabastres *coteries*, or the designations journeymen give each other, the journeyman carpenters of the *devoir* created the Fédération Compagnonnique des Métiers du Bâtiment, a new organization that welcomed, in addition to the *chiens-loups*, the journeyman joiners and locksmiths of

Opposite: **Work in progress on the Royal Portal of Chartres Cathedral. Heirs to the traditions of the builders of the great cathedrals, journeymen are often asked to participate in the monuments' maintenance and restoration.**

Far left: **Headquarters of the Association Ouvrière des Compagnons du Devoir in Paris**

Left: **National headquarters of the Fédération Compagnonnique des Métiers du Bâtiment, formerly the chapter house of the *soubises* carpenters of La Villette**

the *devoir de liberté* (known as *gavots*) and, increasingly, other professional craft groups established for the purpose.

Since that time, the Fédération Compagnonnique has been composed of four societies: Société des Compagnons Charpentiers des *Devoirs* du Tour de France (rites of Solomon and Soubise combined), the fellowship from which the federation grew; Société des Compagnons Maçons-Tailleurs de Pierre des *Devoirs* du Tour de France (rite of Master Jacques); Société des Compagnons Passants *Bons Drilles* Couvreurs, Zingueurs, Plombiers et Plâtriers (rite of Father Soubise); Société des Compagnons Menuisiers et Serruriers du *Devoir de Liberté* (*gavots;* rite of Solomon). It is also worth noting the presence of a few journeyman farriers of the *devoir* in the Fédération Compagnonnique.

What is unique to this *compagnonnage* is that each of its constituent societies has its own Tour de France as well as autonomous control of its chapter houses while participating in the common administration of the federation. Furthermore, each craft inducts its members using whatever rite it chooses. Every year, a general assembly brings together delegates from the various regional headquarters to elect an overall head of the organization, the président national.

The Fédération Compagnonnique solicits applications from young men who have earned a CAP (*Certificat d'aptitude profesionnelle*) or a BEP (*Brevet d'etudes professionelles*). If they pass some qualifying tests, they must then agree to abide by

the group's rules, which apply throughout France. Like the two other organizations, the Fédération Compagnonnique des Métiers du Bâtiment attaches particular importance to the educational progress of its young workers. As with the Association Ouvrière, it consists of many chapters that are organized into regional federations. It is on cordial terms with the Union Compagnonnique, but its relations with the Association Ouvrière are sometimes cooler, for the Association's activities in the postwar years remain controversial. Maintaining close ties with journeymen associations throughout Europe, the Fédération Compagnonnique des Métiers du Bâtiment is currently the only French journeyman organization affiliated with the Confédération des Compagnonnages Européens.

THE TOUR DE FRANCE

*rimard* (slang for "road"), *brillant* (radiant): two French words that, through the ages, have been used to characterize the famous Tour de France, the professional journey of enlightenment and discovery sponsored for young workers by the *compagnonnage*.

Despite profound changes in the world of labor, the Tour de France retains all the advantages associated from the past. Passing from city to city, today's itinerant youngsters can still profit from this voyage that lasts several years, during which they can deepen their understanding of their craft and, beyond that, of their own character.

istud bre... ...cnnu in
...ueneu... ...ulandus... 8 hu
...t...peruus de... ...beu
...disputande

istud en ...piel...viteru
Scī...phanaone...in
...uiuus

Vesci les ligemenr de le glere de trvay de saint esteune.
Deseure est une glize a double charole. R...iurs vehoncort...truvve...

The Light of the Cathedrals: Chartres

Above: **Detail of a stained-glass window, Notre-Dame de Chartres. Chartres was a popular stop among journeymen of all crafts on the Tour de France.**

Opposite: **Page from the notebook of the thirteenth-century architect Villard d'Harnoncourt**

CHARTRES

"Chartres is a small town situated on steep hills. Several of its streets are called hillocks, which suits them quite well: they are impassable for conveyances. Aside from the cathedral, there are no monuments worthy of note." Thus did Agricol Perdiguier, in his *Mémoires d'un Compagnon*, describe the city of Chartres, where, in 1826, he was certified in a solemn ceremony a "finished" journeyman. Chartres has never been considered the most important city on the Tour de France. Aside from the *gavots*, very few societies had a chapter house there. We nonetheless begin our Tour de France itinerary with this city because the sublime building to which it is home is a sacred monument dear to all *compagnons*, the only structure that Agricol Perdiguier deemed worthy of mention: the cathedral.

The Heirs of the Cathedral Builders

Many texts describe journeymen of the Tour de France as the worthy heirs and spiritual sons of the cathedral builders. From the Association Ouvrière des Compagnons du Devoir to the Fédération Compagnonnique des Devoirs Unis, all French journeyman families are in agreement on this point.

Many curious geometric signs are engraved on old masonry blocks and wooden beams, marks of the various journeymen; visitors to the cathedral will discover stars, circles, triangles, arrows, set-squares, compasses, and many other symbols dear to these craftsmen. In the eyes of some, such simple visible marks in wood and stone prove that the people capable of building these masterpieces of royal art came from *compagnonnage*.

It is clear that cathedral construction sites attracted workers trained in the skills needed to build and decorate these edifices. Local populations regarded traveling artisans, exempted from local guild control during their stays, as *étrangers* (for-

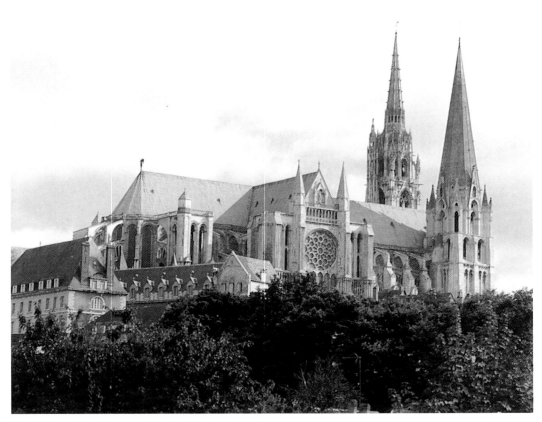

Preceding pages: **Stained glass from the cathedral of Chartres, "A blue . . . so moving it could be from another world,"** *Tourangeau le Disciple de la Lumière* **(The Disciple of Light from Touraine)**

Left: **The cathedral of Chartres enjoys a special prestige. A monument of stone and glass, it makes a profound impression on the many pilgrims who come to admire it.**

eigners) and *passants* (itinerants), descriptive terms of considerable importance in the history of *compagnonnage*. A pilgrimage site for all Christian people, Chartres is, for journeyman glaziers, a sacred place, a temple boasting nearly two thousand square meters of stained-glass windows. After admiring the carved portals and porches, visitors can proceed to the interior, where a marvelous world of symbols and legends awaits them.

Among the masterpieces of stained glass that illuminate the cathedral, the windows devoted to the tree of Jesse, the childhood of Christ, and the Passion are of unequaled perfection. In the periodical *Le Compagnonnage* (August 1977), the Disciple of Light from Touraine, a journeyman glazier of the Devoirs Unis, expresses his admiration for the work in glass: "The scene of the Passion stands out against a background of supernatural blue, not even the most precious sapphires could compete with this blue, which is so moving it could be from another world."

While rational and functional as buildings, cathedrals are also mystical and symbolic vessels. In this, they are analogous to *compagnonnage*, for each, behind its facade, conveys a message of fraternity and fosters a love of the beautiful, a philosophy that situates the worker at the heart of the great construction sites.

Chartres is the cathedral of guilds and crafts, an astonishing church that boasts some ten thousand painted and sculpted figures. Better than any history book, the cathedral brings to life the Middle Ages by revealing its most profound reflections to anyone willing to explore its vast extent, from east to west, from north to south, from bottom to top.

The cathedral is an invitation to travel down a path leading to the heart of a spirituality. In *Le Compagnonnage* (September 1984), *La Volonté de Vouvray* (The Willful One from Vouvray), an itinerant journeyman stonecutter of the *devoir*, openly expresses his feelings and convictions:

> Symbolically, a man who prays on his knees in the half light of a Romanesque cathedral humbles himself, and, with joined hands pointing toward infinity, extends his arms toward the Creator. Like the arches perfectly joined and secured above his head. Like the towers that resemble two imploring arms. From the half light of Romanesque cathedrals, with their few small windows, man humbles himself in the radiating light of the windows of Gothic cathedrals. And all the art, the entire building, becomes radiant. And man surpasses himself, goes beyond himself, elevates himself toward his Creator with the help of the Faith that guides him. The works in stone and wood, the paintings and sculptures do more than radiate. They blaze. They reveal the magnificence beyond the work. It is art at its peak.

Whether they are believers or not, journeymen are indeed the descendants of the cathedral builders. To be convinced of this, one need only hear them talk about the cathedrals in Chartres, Amiens, Reims, Strasbourg, and Paris. In their plans, sculptures, and stained-glass windows, in all their masterpieces, situated both inside and outside, the *compagnons* of today still learn to decipher the messages transmitted by the men they

Two contemporary journeyman emblems

Left: **Detail of the colors of the journeyman joiners of the *devoir* (Compagnons Menuisiers du Devoir, or CMDD)**

Right: **Detail of the colors of the journeyman of the *devoirs unis* (the UC stands for Union Compagnonnique)**

consider their elders. This is why the cathedrals figure prominently in the symbolism of *compagnonnage*.

The Labyrinth

The labyrinth in the cathedral of Chartres is, together with those of Amiens and Bayeux, one of the most famous. For Christians unable to visit the Holy Land, the labyrinth offered a substitute rite: they could traverse its entire course on their knees, praying. Composed of mosaic, colored stone, and enamel tiles, the labyrinths are, according to some, signatures inscribed by the builders. Here again, we must evoke the dual nature of all sacred buildings. In addition to their manifest function, the labyrinths also had a symbolic aspect. In the journeyman tradition, they are considered symbols of striving, knowledge, and transmission. When a "traveler" reaches the center, he or she must retrace the course in order to pass on his or her experience, or at least a portion of it, for all pilgrimage trips lead to discoveries nearly impossible to communicate to others. Like the cathedral labyrinths, the Tour de France reveals its lessons only to itinerants who successfully meet all of its challenges.

In the *compagnonnage* of the *devoir*, when a young man is taken on as an aspirant, the sponsoring journeymen give him a symbolic color, or sash, bearing an image of the labyrinth, symbol of the long and difficult but formative course that awaits him on the Tour de France. Proof of the symbolic importance of the labyrinth, this image also appears on the colors of *mères* of journeymen of the *devoir*.

Colors

The term "colors"—*couleurs* in French—designates the ribbons or sashes of specific shapes, cuts, and colors (hence the name) worn by *compagnons* on ceremonial occasions. They often bear emblems of various kinds, applied with an engraved roller when the ribbon is made of silk and with a hot iron when it is made of velvet. For centuries, the colors were worn at various heights, from waist- to hat-level, in accordance with the historical priority of one's craft within *compagnonnage*. Today, the symbolism associated with the colors, notably regarding their placement, has been much simplified. But they remain a sacred attribute for journeymen, for they attest to their level of expertise and title.

The Union Compagnonnique des Devoirs Unis assigns its aspirants a green color, symbolic of hope and perseverance. When he is received as a *compagnon*, he qualifies for a red sash worn over the shoulder. Among other emblems, it bears a radiant delta and a square and compass. When he becomes a "finished" *compagnon*, his colors are enriched with a branch of acacia. *Pays* who have rendered great services to *compagnonnage* are awarded honorary white sashes.

The Fédération Compagnonnique des Métiers du Bâtiment allows each of its affiliated societies to determine the choice and disposition of its colors. Thus *gavots* retain their traditional blue and white ribbons, which they fix to the first buttonhole of their vests. Beginning *compagnons* still sport wide sashes richly embroidered with symbols (square and compass, Justice holding the scales, stars), and bearing their

Opposite: **The labyrinth at Chartres Cathedral**

Left and below: **Even today, a few** *compagnons* **complete some parts of their Tour de France on foot. Here, two young journeyman carpenters on their way to Chartres**

Far left: **Journeyman stonecutter of the Fédération Compagnonnique des Métiers du Bâtiment**

own name and those of the cities where they have satisfied their obligations, accompanied by the corresponding arrival and completion dates. The fringes of its colors are gilded.

The colors of the Association Ouvrière des Compagnons du Devoir are velvet sashes branded with its emblem and symbols of the cities through which the journeyman has passed. Attendants at the reception ceremony of a *mère* can also have a commemorative brand impressed on their sash. The colors initially given to aspirants bear images of the labyrinth and of the tower of Babel; other symbols are applied as their trips proceed.

In order to distinguish the various crafts, the Association Ouvrière has imposed a universal color code. Blue is used only for wood-related crafts, and red only for *pays* practicing iron-related crafts, for they must master fire. Yellow, the color of wheat, is worn by bakers and pastry chefs. Green is attributed to artisans who work with leather and fabric. As for masons, stonecutters, roofers, and plaster workers, their sashes are cream-colored.

Finally, it is worth noting a point of agreement among all three *compagnonnages:* all the *mères* on the Tour de France wear symbolic white ribbons.

The Great City: Paris

PARIS

𝕿his great and beautiful city, its population exceeding that of several departments combined, is the residence of kings, of princes, of the elite, of intelligence. It is the seat of government, the head of France, the theater of revolutions. It is here that talent emerges and shines, flights of genius, the sciences, the arts, all manner of surprises. . . . How beautiful it is, with its quays, its boulevards, its Champs-Élysées, its public squares, its vast gardens, its many monuments, its rich parks! Paris certainly deserves our admiration. Even so, I am struck by a painful contrast. This beautiful place is, for young travelers like ourselves, less hospitable than many others.

Thus did Paris appear through the eyes of Agricol Perdiguier in the first decades of the nineteenth century. In all likelihood, his ambivalence was shared by the vast majority of young itinerants discovering the capital for the first time. Paris was the only stop on the Tour de France that was designated a *grande ville* (great city), a phrase that appears frequently in journeyman songs of the period. Inevitably, the presence of so many workers in so large a city entailed tensions of a kind found nowhere else on the Tour, which explains Perdiguier's initial impression that the place was less hospitable than one might have wished. Still, yesterday as today, it took only a few days for the considerable charm and interest of the "great city" to become apparent.

Paris and the *Compagnons* of the Tour de France

Like Lyon, the city of Paris would require a book for itself alone. Everywhere, *compagnonnage* is present. There is not a single Parisian arrondissement that doesn't harbor a vestige of journeyman culture either engraved in matter or inscribed in

Opposite: **The Eiffel Tower, a masterpiece of journeyman expertise**

Above: **The "forest" of beams supporting the roof above the vaults of Notre-Dame de Paris**

Commemorative plaque attached to the central king-post of Notre-Dame. Note the emblem and symbols of the journeyman carpenters of the *devoir de liberté*.

Opposite, left: **Photograph of Eugène Milon, known as *Guépin le Soutien de Salomon* (The Stay of Solomon), wearing the Saint Andrew's Cross of Freemasonry. Principal *levageur* (contractor-hoister) of the Eiffel Tower, he was later placed in charge of its maintenance and public amenities.**

Opposite, right: **Erection of the Eiffel Tower**

memory. From the Eiffel Tower to the Invalides, from Notre-Dame to the Opéra, *compagnonnage* recalls grandiose enterprises signed by the children of all rites.

From December 1951 to April 1952, the Musée des Arts et Traditions Populaires, for the first time in France, paid well-deserved homage to *compagnonnage* by organizing in the Palais Chaillot an important exhibition devoted to it. The title of this memorable show still resonates with solemn gratitude: "Paris and the *Compagnons* of the Tour de France."

Traditions and Legends

Even today, some journeymen maintain that it was in Paris that the *compagnonnage* received its rule from the hands of the Templars (Solomon being the common denominator of the two institutions) when the latter were building their residence in what had formerly been a *marais*, or marsh, a word still used to designate a certain quarter in Paris. Some doubt the validity of this story, although a painting exists dating from 1480, entitled *The Siege of Rhodes*, which represents journeyman carpenters and stonecutters being inducted by the grand master of the order of Saint John of Jerusalem, which received the heritage of the Templars after that order's trial and dissolution. In this realm of legend there are many such tales relating to the construction of Notre-Dame de Paris and the Sainte-Chapelle.

The Sainte-Chapelle

Erected between 1243 and 1248 by Pierre de Montreuil to house relics from the Crown of Thorns and the True Cross, the Sainte-Chapelle is a masterpiece of thirteenth-century architecture and construction. A very beautiful journeyman story holds that its basic design was conceived by a young journeyman stonecutter of the *saint devoir*. Even if this story is false, the *compagnonnage* is associated with the building because journeymen of the *devoir de liberté*—*indiens* and *étrangers*—played important roles in its mid-nineteenth-century restoration under the direction of Jean-Baptiste Lassus. Henri Georges (1818–1887), known as *Angevin l'Enfant du Génie* (The Child of Genius from Anjou), fashioned its brilliant new spire. Furthermore, the journeyman Hérard, known as *La Vertu de Malicorne* (The Virtuous One from Malicorne), supervised the stonecutters working at the site.

The "Forest" of Notre-Dame

Completed between 1260 and 1370, the extraordinary timber support system for the roof above the stone vaults of Notre-Dame required the wood of at least eight hundred oaks—a veritable forest, hence its nickname. A visitor to this part of the building will discover, here and there, old journeyman marks. Above all, attention will be drawn to a small plaque attached to the central king-post above the crossing. Engraved on a silver-plated surface, one reads:

To the glory of the great architect of the universe
This spire was made in the year MDCCCLIX
M. VIOLLET-LE-DUC
Being architect
Of the cathedral
By BELLU
Entre[preneur] carpenter
GEORGES
Being *gâcheur*
of the journeyman carpenters
of the *devoir de liberté*.

The Protocol of Paris

The almost exclusive employment of journeymen of the *devoir de liberté* for the restoration projects at Notre-Dame and the Sainte-Chapelle may be surprising. Were the journeyman carpenters of Soubise any less competent? Certainly not, as the two rites are regarded as equally skilled. The predominance of children of Solomon on the teams assembled by Viollet-le-Duc and Lassus was dictated by the protocol of Paris. Signed in 1848, this agreement was designed to ensure that *indiens* and *soubises* would each receive a fair share of the employment relating to construction and restoration work in the capital.

The protocol had the great advantage of precluding conflict between the two rival organizations. The *indiens* were allotted the Left Bank and the island of the Cité, while the *soubises* were given exclusive rights to projects located on the Right Bank.

This explains the presence of carpenters of the *devoir de liberté* at Notre-Dame, the Sainte-Chapelle, and the towers of the Conciergerie. For the same reason, they were largely responsible some years later for construction of the Eiffel Tower. As for carpenters of the *devoir, bons drilles* (good fellows) of Father Soubise, they completed, in conformity with the protocol, the restoration of the timber armature supporting the roof of the Hôtel de Ville as well as construction of the iron roof supports of the Grand Palais.

Construction of the Eiffel Tower

In addition to the spires of Notre-Dame and the Sainte-Chapelle, there is another, more celebrated and innovative one that rises majestically into the Parisian sky: the Eiffel Tower. A formidable challenge essayed within the framework of the Exposition Universelle of 1889, the gigantic iron spire designed by the engineer Gustave Eiffel was completed thanks to the talents of Eugène Milon, known as *Guépin le Soutien de Salomon* (The Stay of Solomon). Milon was an exceptional *levageur*, or contractor-hoister; he had worked previously with the Société Eiffel, notably on construction of the audacious viaducts at Tardes and Garabit. Milon, with some forty journeyman carpenters, mostly *indiens* but also a few *soubises*, successfully completed the tower, a task judged impossible by the many critics of the project, including such prominent figures of the day as writers Alexandre Dumas, Guy de Maupassant, and Armand Sully Prudhomme, as well as the architect

Above: **Plaque on the Eiffel Tower
honoring the journeymen who worked
on its construction**

Opposite: **Portrait of Viollet-le-Duc,**
photographed by Nadar

Right: **Sainte-Chapelle, Paris**

Charles Garnier, who had collaborated with journeymen during construction of the new Opéra (1862–74).

Work on the tower commenced on January 26, 1887, and on March 31, 1889, Gustave Eiffel was finally able to unfurl a tricolor flag from the tower's summit. This fantastic project was carried out by a few journeyman carpenters who managed to complete their mission without an electric crane, using only their arms, hand-winches, and hoisting gear, and they did so without any fatalities, despite the many dangers entailed by the work.

On March 25, 1984, in the presence of Jacques Chirac, then mayor of Paris, a group of journeymen honored their brother-predecessors with a commemorative plaque, its text reminding visitors of the crucial role played by the *compagnonnage* in the erection of this monumental masterpiece: "Honor and glory to Eugène Milon known as The Stay of Solomon from Guêpe, journeyman carpenter of the *devoir de liberté,* 1859–1917, and To the journeymen of the two *devoirs,* who under his direction between January 26, 1887, and March 31, 1889, erected the Eiffel Tower."

The Eiffel Tower is also a symbol of the reconciliation of iron and wood, which had long been kept distinct in journeyman tradition. It was not easy for Eugène Milon to convince his fellow carpenters to abandon "noble" wood in favor of a material that some of them referred to disparagingly as scrap iron. It was a journeyman blacksmith of the *devoir,* the *pays* Larivière, known as *Beauceron la Belle Conscience* (The Beautiful Conscience from Beauce), who forged, using a

steam-hammer, the large bolts that secure the bedplates of the tower's four corners.

From Garnier's Opéra to the Pont Alexandre-III

When walking past the Paris Opéra, known as the Palais Garnier in honor of its architect, journeymen of the Tour de France are likely to remember one of their own who was the project's true stone dresser. In effect, the cutting and dressing of all of the stone used in the building was supervised by the journeyman Jansaud, known to itinerant journeyman stone-cutters of the *devoir* by the symbolic name *La Prudence de Draguignan* (The Prudent One from Draguignan).

In the late nineteenth century, the capital, wishing to heal the many scars left by the Franco-Prussian War and the Commune, was gripped by a fever for building. In this frenzy of reconstruction, Paris covered itself with remarkable apartment and office buildings of dressed stone. In several cases, the preparation of their masonry was entrusted to the journeyman Leturgeon, known as *La Fidélité de Vouvray* (The Faithful One from Vouvray). Restoration of the Hôtel de Ville was placed under the authority of the stone dresser Maréchal, known as *La Franchise de Grenoble* (The Candid One from Grenoble). The journeyman Cornette, *La Franchise de Pont-à-Mousson* (The Candid One from Pont-à-Mousson), was similarly entrusted with the Gare Saint-Lazare. The *coterie* Boucher, known as *Franc-Coeur d'Avallon* (The Sincere Heart from Avallon), did likewise for the Grand Palais. In 1889, the con-

Preceding pages: ***The Reconciliation of the Journeymen***, an 1872 lithograph inspired by the assembly of some ten thousand journeymen of all the *devoirs* in Paris at the Place des Vosges on March 21, 1848

Left: ***The Berryer***, "masterpiece" presented by the journeyman carpenters of the *soubise* to a famous Parisian lawyer who defended them after the great strike of 1845

Right: **Detail from a reception piece of a journeyman *ébéniste* (maker of luxury furniture)**

tractor Letellier, looking for a stone dresser capable of overseeing the cutting of the precise masonry of the Pont Alexandre-III, selected Jean Galineau, known as *Joli Coeur de Coutras* (The Pleasing Heart from Coutras).

From the vast construction site that was Paris under Baron Haussmann to the laying out of the city's first *métro* lines, journeymen of the stone, wood, and iron crafts had privileged vantage points from which to observe the transformation of the French capital.

Berryer, Lawyer of the *Devoir*

In 1845, the famous Parisian lawyer Pierre-Antoine Berryer defended a group of journeyman carpenters (most of them *soubises*), who were accused of committing violent acts, uttering threats, and calling for work stoppages during the strikes organized that summer by all of the city's carpenters. To ensure their proper defense, journeymen of the two rites did not hesitate to join forces. Finding their cause just, Berryer and the four lawyers who assisted him refused to accept a fee.

As an expression of gratitude, in 1847 the journeyman carpenters of the *devoir* gave Berryer a remarkable demonstration of craft virtuosity that immediately became known as "The Berryer." Fabricated by the Pizargue *coterie*, almost ten feet tall, it is a scale model of a three-story bell tower with a freestanding spiral stair in the center of its second story. The lawyer kept it in his Parisian office until his death, after which it was returned to the *soubises* journeymen. Since the merger of the two carpentry rites in 1945, it has been the property of

the journeyman carpenters of the *devoirs*, who keep it at their headquarters in Paris.

The Faubourg Saint-Antoine

The memory of Agricol Perdiguier still exists at several sites in Paris. In Père-Lachaise cemetery, flowers are kept on his tomb by the journeymen who come to pay him homage there every All Saints' Day. *La Vertu d'Avignon* (The Virtuous One from Avignon) was, above all, a joiner of the faubourg Saint-Antoine. Journeyman of all rites and well-known personalities like French statesmen Jules Ferry and Léon Gambetta came to meet the reformer of *compagnonnage* in his house in the heart of the faubourg Saint-Antoine.

For centuries, this neighborhood was home to joiners and *ébénistes*, or makers of luxury furniture, who belonged to the city's guilds. Raoul Vergez evoked the special place occupied by this part of the city in the journeyman heritage:

The faubourg is not a dead guild community. Certainly not! Everywhere there are people sawing and planing, the planing machines rotate, throughout the little courtyards the hum of turners [*toupies*] on the fourth and fifth floors can be heard. . . . How much longer will Louis XV, Empire, and Renaissance pieces be restored on the rue de la Main d'Or, at the Marché d'Aligre and as far as the end of the rue de Reuilly? Wood slicing, wood peeling, and wood lamination were conceived and realized in this vast woodworking laboratory. The French Revolution, with the brewer Santerre, the coup d'état of 1851,

Left: **Agricol Perdiguier toward the end of his life**

Right: **"The Viannay," 18'8" h. Made entirely of walnut, this "masterpiece" made by the *indiens* is now owned by the journeyman carpenters of the *devoir* (FCMB).**

with representative Baudin, who showed how a delegate could die for 25 francs a day, and also 45,000 joiners voting in 1848 for one of their own, winning him a seat in the Parlement: Agricol Perdiguier. It was the extraordinary influence of the workers in the faubourg Saint-Antoine that, in the storms of history, forced the destiny of Paris.

—Raoul Vergez, *Les Compagnons d'aujourd'hui,* 1973

Nowhere better than in this *faubourg* does the image of the journeyman engaged in politics and social activities, without neglecting his craft, take on its full dimensions. Like other quarters of Paris, however, the Saint-Antoine is changing: several of its old workshops, rich in memories, disappear every year. Today's journeymen know that the incomparable workers' community that once flourished here, a fraternity of the wood crafts that left its mark on the city's history, is gone forever.

From the Place des Vosges to the Dome of the Invalides

Perdiguier's militant advocacy of a merger of the old *devoirs* found its theater in Paris, a platform from which he could be heard throughout France. Books, lectures, trips, and meetings punctuated the life of *La Vertu d'Avignon,* who divided his time between politics (which bought him exile in 1851) and the cause of *compagnonnage.* Within one day, Perdiguier's dream became a reality. On March 21, 1848, in the Place des Vosges, ten thousand journeymen of all the *devoirs* gathered in an expression of fraternal unity, then marched through Paris

before being received at the Hôtel de Ville by the provisional revolutionary government. This ephemeral merger was immortalized by Perdiguier in a 1872 lithograph entitled *The Reconciliation of the Journeymen.*

Our account of "journeyman" Paris would be incomplete if we did not mention the Hôtel des Invalides. For journeyman carpenters of the *soubise*, it is associated with the memory of Nicolas Fourneau, known as *Angevin la Cour Céleste* (The Celestial Court from Anjou), who supposedly helped to complete the dome of the domed church. We should also note that the tomb of Napoleon inside the church, a masterpiece of stonework and stone-finishing, was realized by François Guibert, itinerant journeyman stonecutter of the *devoir.* Contemporary *compagnonnage* has also left its mark on the capital. The famous glass pyramids of the Louvre are perfect symbols of a *compagnonnage* that has managed to adapt to the demands of the modern world.

The National Headquarters

Just a few steps from the Hôtel de Ville in Paris, to the side of the church of Saint-Gervais, is the national headquarters of the Association Ouvrière des Compagnons du Devoir. *Au Compagnon fini* ("At the finished *compagnon*") is the symbolic name of this house of the Tour de France, where young itinerants lodge during their Parisian sojourns. The organization's various administrative offices are also the editorial offices of its official publication, *Compagnon du devoir.* Just down the street is the Librairie du Compagnonnage, a bookshop specializing

F. MÉAULLE

Opposite: **Illustration from *Le Petit Parisien*, 1900, the "Viannay" being transported from the Exposition Universelle to the chapter house on rue Mabillon**

Far left: **Tomb of Agricol Perdiguier in Père-Lachaise cemetery, Paris**

Left: **Journeyman mark of "CHARTTRE LE PARISIIN" [*sic*] from 1648 on the spiral stair in the church of Saint-Gilles du Gard**

in publications relating to *compagnonnage* and whose clientele extends throughout France.

The Fédération Compagnonnique des Métiers du Bâtiment is situated in the nineteenth arrondissement of Paris. An important center of *soubises* journeyman carpenters, La Villette has been under the control of the Fédération since the merger of the *indiens* and the *soubises* in 1945. A few feet from the national headquarters is the restaurant Aux Arts et Sciences Réunis, a gathering place for journeymen; all visitors are cordially received there, and during their meal they can soak up the atmosphere of journeyman sociability that prevails. As a friend to journeymen, they can also admire the great "masterpieces" of carpentry produced in the nineteenth century by both *soubises* and *indiens*. The "Mazerolle," the "Viannay," the "Légendre," and the "Berryer" are all on display here in a small room adjacent to the restaurant.

Another place of pilgrimage dear to journeyman carpenters of the *devoirs* is situated on the famous rue Mabillon in the sixth arrondissement. The old chapter house of the *indiens* on that street has been transformed into a bookstore-cum-museum of *compagnonnage*, adjacent to the also famous restaurant Les Charpentiers, where you can dine surrounded by "masterpieces" and diplomas.

Recently, the Union Compagnonnique des Devoirs Unis moved its national headquarters from Paris to a magnificent, newly restored residence in Versailles, dedicated in September 1989. But the Union has not abandoned Paris, for in 1988 the city government gave it a building to restore in the very heart of the Halles quarter near the Forum gardens and the church of Saint-Eustache. This is destined to become the organization's Paris chapter house.

A Parisian tour would be incomplete without mentioning the celebrated Fondation de Coubertin, located about thirty miles southwest of the city in Saint-Rémy-lès-Chevreuse. First considered in 1950, in discussions between the journeyman Jean Bernard, first counselor of the Association Ouvrière, and Yvonne de Coubertin, the niece of Pierre de Coubertin, the foundation was officially established only in 1973, after several years of preparation. In facilities on the grounds of the splendid Château de Coubertin, which holds a library, classrooms, study rooms, and studios, the foundation sponsors workshops for journeymen of the *devoir*. The standards of its courses, which encompass practice, theory, and history, are very high. In a few years, the Fondation de Coubertin has earned a solid reputation, especially as a training center in metalwork and casting.

The Meeting of Hand and Mind: Troyes

TROYES

Our city of Troyes, capital in Champagne
D'Urbain of François Roux, this last journeyman
How many famous men have left for the country
Coming from your *faubourgs*, simply, without fuss.
In Hôtel de Mauroy, a celebrated museum of tools
Celebrates "workers' thought,"
In your house of wood, tiles, and stone
Aspirant, journeyman, follow tradition.

> —From the song "Trois Villes Encor"(Three towns more),
> composed by Pierre Morin, known as *Pierre le Saintonge*
> (Pierre from Saintonge), 1977

This verse from the song by a journeyman joiner of the *devoir*, deftly brings to the fore two prominent features of *compagnonnage* in Troyes. Troyes was the birthplace of the famous joiner François Roux, author of a celebrated "masterpiece." The city also houses a unique museum of which the Association Ouvrière des Compagnons du Devoir du Tour de France has reason to be proud: the Maison de l'Outil et de la Pensée Ouvrière (House of Tools and Workers' Thought).

The Ordinance of Charles VI

The departmental seat of the Aube occupies an especially important place in the history of *compagnonnage*, since an ordinance issued in 1420 by King Charles VI concerning the cobblers of the city contains the oldest known reference to the Tour de France: "Several journeymen and workers of the said craft, of various languages and nations, came and went from town to town to work, learn, experience, see, and know one another." One could scarcely better characterize the principal goal of the Tour de France: to travel in order to perfect a craft. This objective is still embraced by today's young itinerants in

Opposite: **Hôtel Jean de Mauroy, a superb sixteenth-century residence recently restored by journeymen of the *devoir*, now houses the celebrated Maison de l'Outil et de la Pensée Ouvrière (House of Tools and Workers' Thought).**

Right: **A two-beaked anvil**

Right: **Masterpiece of François Roux, known as** *François le Champagne* **(François from Champagne), journeyman joiner of the** *devoir*. **Consisting of 17,700 pieces of wood, it is a three-dimensional puzzle, for it can be dismantled and rebuilt. It was restored in 1955–56 by Pierre Sudre, known as** *Pierre l'Ariégois* **(Pierre from Ariége).**

Far right: **Portrait of François Roux (1809–1865)**

the Association Ouvrière des Compagnons du Devoir, the only journeyman organization in Troyes.

François Roux, known as *François le Champagne*

Born in Troyes on March 8, 1809, into a family of weavers, François Roux followed the Tour de France and was received as a journeyman joiner of the *devoir* in Marseilles in 1833, under the symbolic name *François le Champagne* (François from Champagne). After completion of his Tour, he returned to Marseilles, where he settled permanently and opened a workshop. Although he could have been discussed in the chapter on that city, his journeyman name has forever linked him to the city of Troyes, which claims him as one of its glorious children.

François le Champagne owes his inclusion in the journeyman pantheon to a fantastic "masterpiece" that he made between 1851 and 1859 to win glory for his organization. Composed of 17,700 pieces fabricated from all known woods of the period, it is the model of a temple some five and a half feet high. A type of puzzle (it can be dismantled and rebuilt), it demonstrated his complete mastery of all the difficulties and subtleties of the *trait*. From 1860 to 1862, *François le Champagne* traveled across France with his admirable work to bring honor to his organization and glory to *compagnonnage*. In every city he visited, all the local civil and religious dignitaries joined with journeymen of all the *devoirs* in their admiration of this "masterpiece" and its author. Perdiguier discerned

an aspect of the piece not anticipated by Roux, who had conceived it as a definitive demonstration of the superiority of the *devoirants* over the *gavots*. Here is what Perdiguier wrote:

> It is a remarkable work that the joiners of the *devoir* transport from city to city, exhibiting it to all gazes in order to win the glory that is rightly theirs, and, in addition, to spur a love of work and of craft among the working class. But this work, which at the start was only a weapon inspired by bellicose thoughts, something meant to elevate some and cast down others, to deepen the abyss separating the two rival organizations, has become, thanks to the modesty of "the one from Champagne," its author, who accompanies it everywhere, to the great advantage of the organization that paid for it, and also, let it be said, of the eruption of new ideas in *compagnonnage*, an occasion for reconciliation and fraternization. When the "masterpiece" is exhibited in a city, everyone visits it, journeymen of the *devoir* and journeymen of the *devoir de liberté* see one another, speak to one another, acknowledge its merit. Hands are shaken, hearts are reconciled, and in the end the work of one organization is regarded as a collective work that does honor to all journeyman organizations.

As Perdiguier attests, *François le Champagne*, through his exceptional "masterpiece," helped to pacify the *devoirs* at a time when they were likely to quarrel at the slightest provocation. After having visited several cities, François Roux returned to Marseilles, where he fell victim to cholera in 1865. The journeymen moved his "masterpiece" to Tours. Having suf-

Medal made by the journeyman Jean Bernard as an homage to the Jesuit priest Paul Feller, at whose instigation the Maison de l'Outil et de la Pensée Ouvrière was founded

fered the ravages of time, in 1955–56 it was restored by the journeyman Sudre, known as *Pierre l'Ariégois* (Pierre from Ariége). It is now owned by the Association Ouvrière des Compagnons du Devoir du Tour de France.

Paul Feller, a Jesuit in the Service of Apprenticeship

Born in 1913, Paul Feller entered the Jesuit seminary in Lyon and was ordained a priest in 1947. Named in 1952 to the *action populaire*, which provides services to the underprivileged, in Vanves, he there became interested in manual apprenticeship, organizing several colloquia on the subject. Actively pursuing his interest, he became an apprentice roofer and then, under the aegis of the Institut Catholique des Arts et Métiers, he learned the craft of forging in Lille.

In that city he began to assemble what rapidly became an impressive collection of old tools, seeking them out tirelessly from iron-mongers, in old workshops, and in antique shops. Wanting to become better acquainted with *compagnonnage*, he completed a Tour de France organized by the Association Ouvrière des Compagnons du Devoir.

Under the terms of a 1969 agreement between this organization and the Jesuits, all writings and artifacts gathered by the latter pertaining to the French craft traditions were handed over to the *devoir*. The result was the Maison de l'Outil et de la Pensée Ouvrière in Troyes (House of Tools and Workers' Thought). Thanks to this new museum, a larger public is able to reap the rewards of Father Feller's efforts. Feller, who was

fond of saying "I would like to be a messenger of joy for the young," died in 1979.

The Maison de l'Outil et de la Pensée Ouvrière

The Hôtel de Mauroy in Troyes is a beautiful sixteenth-century building, entirely restored by journeymen of the *devoir* of the Tour de France. It contains the Maison de l'Outil et de la Pensée Ouvrière, which consists of a fascinating museum of old tools as well as an impressive library of materials relating to the world of work and *compagnonnage*. Several "masterpieces" by journeymen of the *devoir* are also on view there, adding considerably to the interest of the collection. The expression "*la main est esprit*" (hand and mind are one) here assumes its full symbolic import. Father Feller never tired of evoking the special character of the Maison de l'Outil:

> Mauroy is for me the site of a double struggle: between adults who have a craft and those who do not; and between adolescents who choose a true apprenticeship and those who do not. Mauroy is for me a place where the accelerated pace of the schism between manual and non-manual labor slows. Mauroy is for me the most modest place there is, and on leaving it one should feel, if not humble, then a bit more modest.

These sentences, pronounced before a few itinerant journeymen of the Association Ouvrière, describe feelings that will be shared by many visitors to the museum.

The fascinating displays in the Maison de l'Outil et de la Pensée Ouvrière (House of Tools and Workers' Thought) are attracting more and more visitors.

The emblem consisting of a superimposed square and compass still appears on journeyman colors.

Above: **Colors of the Association Ouvrière**

Opposite, left: **Pendulum levels**

Opposite, right: **Compasses for measuring thickness, used by stone dressers and carpenters**

Officially inaugurated in 1974, the Maison de l'Outil et de la Pensée Ouvrière receives thousands of visitors each year, proof of its deserved renown. Hammers, compasses, adzes, anvils, howels, pickaxes, cleaving irons, hatchets, *jabloires* (tools for cutting crozes), and *boutoirs* (knives used by curriers, farriers, and cobblers) are admirably presented. In addition to the traditional crafts of *compagnonnage*, the museum also features displays pertaining to professions that are unknown or too often ignored, such as chair making, upholstering, and repair. The library, which boasts hundreds of volumes, some quite rare, is a precious resource for anyone interested in the workers' traditions so dear to Father Feller. On June 11, 1991, the president of the French Republic, François Mitterrand, dedicated its new quarters, rooms that had been restored over the preceding eight years.

Discussion of this high place of *compagnonnage* would be incomplete without mentioning that an ever-younger public is discovering the beauty and virtues of the world of craft in the wonderful rooms of the Maison de l'Outil et de la Pensée Ouvrière. It is indeed fulfilling the mission assigned by its founder, who hoped it would attract "young people endowed with intelligence and heart" to manual crafts.

Square and Compass

Two tools, more than any others, have come to symbolize *compagnonnage*. Much has been written about the square and the compass—most of it, unfortunately, by authors who are unfamiliar with the realities of the craft skills involved.

Because the superimposed square and compass also figure in Masonic symbolism, some writers have hastily confused the two institutions. It is true that the Temple of Solomon and the figure of Hiram are common to both journeyman and Masonic legends; signs of recognition and "*les trois points*" are still used in some journeyman societies. But it would be erroneous, given the distinct identities of the two institutions, to maintain that *compagnonnage* is a variant of Freemasonry. It is true that, like Agricol Perdiguier, Lucien Blanc, and Raoul Vergez, some journeymen on the Tour de France have frequented, and continue to frequent, various French Masonic lodges. But this is separate from their obligations and identity as journeymen; their Masonic affiliation is the result of a strictly individual choice relating to that institution's initiatory challenges.

The most fundamental point of difference between journeyman and Masonic organizations is that membership in the former is restricted to individuals seriously committed to mastering a craft. Work with certain materials is the distinctive sign of all journeymen on the Tour de France. The existence of a *compagnonnage* under the tutelage of Freemasonry is without historical foundation. Having made these clarifications, we can address the meaning of the square and compass in journeyman symbolism.

The square is, above all, an instrument of control. Many medieval images show stonecutters verifying the accuracy and quality of their work with this tool, thus associating the material that one seeks to embellish with an enlightened hand. As

for the compass, it is primarily the tool of a designer, one who knows how to conceptualize and orient work on the site. Among *indiens*, it is traditional to present a silver compass to fellow journeymen who, through the quality of their work, have done honor to the *compagnonnage*.

Square and compass equal matter and spirit: such is the duality that each skilled journeyman strives to make one. For these workers, hand is spirit, and hand is mind. Journeymen have long been held in low esteem by those who are ill-informed about the world of craft. The square-and-compass emblem is intended to indicate to young workers that mind and hand are inseparable. Before realizing their "masterpiece," candidates for the status of journeyman must plan and conceptualize it. The beauty of such work is the result of prolonged intellectual effort that is nourished by manual experience. Hand and mind must not be separated, or worse, set against one another, for the goal is maximum self-realization. This is the great lesson of *compagnonnage*.

Men of the So-called Manual Craft

If there is a way to become a man by mastering a so-called manual craft, this way of becoming a man entails reaching thresholds, and such thresholds are common to all crafts. Having passed them, one becomes a man by becoming a worker; to enter the craft, one has to delve into oneself, into the deepest part of oneself. . . .

Happy is he who possesses two tools and before expressing a preference for one over the other, chooses the tool that will permit him to pose and perhaps help him to solve the question: Why and how does a man become a man by mastering a so-called manual craft?

—Paul Feller

The City of Jean le Lorrain: Nancy

NANCY

Among journeymen, Nancy has never been an obligatory stop on the Tour de France. This is largely because of the troubled history of Lorraine. But Nancy has a special appeal for journeymen in the iron crafts, for it boasts exceptional architecture and metalwork.

At the instigation of King Stanislas I Leszcynski, exiled from Poland and made ruler of Barrois and Lorraine by Louis XV, the city of Meurthe-et-Moselle received remarkable embellishments to its buildings and monuments. In addition to the architect Emmanuel Héré, journeyman metalworkers venerate above all the memory of an audacious and gifted metalworker: Jean Lamour.

Jean Lamour, Metalworker to the King

Born March 26, 1698, the son of a master metalworker, young Jean Lamour had no difficulty obtaining the status of master himself. Following the example of journeymen on the Tour de France, he left his father's workshop to complete his education in the iron-working arts. In Metz and Paris he perfected his skills in design and metalwork. In October 1719, having obtained the status of master, he opened his own workshop in Nancy. After completing various repair and maintenance projects, he began to make a name for himself by fabricating balcony and stair railings for the Château d'Haroué. In 1726, he was named to the honorific post of official metalworker to the city of Nancy. From that point forward, commissions multiplied.

The work produced in Lamour's workshop differed from that produced elsewhere: he used exceptionally thick pieces of metal, produced to his specifications. This innovation, which entailed solving delicate problems in both working and assembly, was the result of a commission for the now famous grilles on Place Stanislas. This project, which would

Opposite: **Jean Lamour, the Amphitrite Fountain on Place Stanislas, Nancy**

Above: **Journeymen, such as this artisan working with gold, regard Nancy as the city of Jean Lamour,** **also known as Jean le Lorrain, a remarkable metalworker. From Place Stanislas to the rue Saint-Julien, the educated eye will find many examples of superb metalwork to admire.**

Left: **Lucien Descaves (pictured here with his wife) is one of very few figures to be awarded the rank and title of honorary journeyman.**

Opposite: **Portrait of Bernard Palissy. Claims that the ceramicist Palissy was a journeyman of the *devoir* rest only on oral tradition. As with many famous individuals for whom similar claims are made, there is a lack of historical documentation to confirm such an assertion.**

be the highlight of Lamour's career, necessitated novel technical solutions, for traditional metalworking techniques would be inadequate for such a monumental design fronting a royal square. To produce the incomparable piece of open-air metallic architecture, he had to trace the shapes on sheets of metal, deftly balancing thick and delicate forms, cut, shape, and assemble them on a supporting armature with such skill that the seams would be all but invisible. Even today, the grilles and gates on Place Stanislas compel the admiration of connoisseurs. Other productions from his hand are equally impressive, for example, the superb railings of the first-floor balconies of the Hôtel de Ville in Nancy and the stair railing in the same building.

Among their many projects, King Stanislas and his architect Héré also set out to embellish the Place de la Carrière, an extension of the Place Royale. Here again, Jean Lamour demonstrated his talent and genius as a metalworker. When he died on June 20, 1771, Jean Lamour was considered the greatest metalworker of his age. He was the first designer and technician capable of realizing metalwork truly architectural in character, an achievement made possible by his integration of large-scale metalwork with masonry.

Some journeyman metalworkers claim him as one of their own. They maintain that his symbolic name was "Jean le Lorrain." However, there is no historical proof of his affiliation with the *compagnonnage du devoir*. Whether a journeyman or not, Jean Lamour remains an important figure for all itinerants who, on their Tour de France, make a point of passing through Nancy to admire the splendid productions of Jean le Lorrain.

Other Celebrated Figures Associated with *Compagnonnage*

Jean Lamour is not the only figure considered to have been a Tour-de-France journeyman. According to oral tradition, the famous ceramicist Bernard Palissy (1508–1590) was initiated into the mysteries of *compagnonnage*. Some journeymen go so far as to advance his symbolic name: *Agenais le Fierté du Devoir* (The Pride of the Devoir from Agen).

Sébastien Le Prestre de Vauban (1633–1707), a noted marshal of France, named commissary general of fortifications in 1678, is also sometimes said to have belonged to the organization of itinerant stonecutters of the *devoir*. Here again, there is no historical documentation to support this claim.

Although Eugène-Emmanuel Viollet-le Duc (1814–1879) worked consistently with journeyman carpenters and stonecutters, he never became a journeyman himself, despite occasional claims to the contrary. Even the assertion that he was awarded the status of honorary journeyman (*compagnon d'honneur*) remains hypothetical until reliable proof is available.

Compagnons d'Honneur

Compagnon d'honneur (honorary journeyman) is a title that, on rare occasions, is conferred upon individuals who do not belong to *compagnonnage* but who have rendered service to the institution, or who have demonstrated their respect and admi-

Opposite: **Portrait of the writer George Sand (1804–1876). A friend of Perdiguier and of *compagnonnage*, and author of the novel *Le Compagnon du tour de France* (The Journeyman of the Tour de France, 1841), Sand was so highly regarded by journeymen that some organizations conferred upon her the status of honorary *mère*.**

Right: **Édouard Herriot (1872–1957). This celebrated politician of the radical party was awarded the title of *compagnon d'honneur* (honorary journeyman) by the journeymen cooks of the city of Lyon, where he served as mayor from 1905 to 1957.**

ration for it. This practice, while no longer current, was used by various journeyman organizations until relatively recent times.

The journalist and writer Lucien Descaves received honorary colors from journeyman farriers of the *devoir* in recognition of his support of the encyclopedia *Les Muses du tour de France,* launched by Abel Boyer, known as *Périgord Coeur Loyal* (The Loyal Heart from Périgord), in 1925. Exceptionally, Descaves was also given the symbolic name *Noble Coeur de Lutèce* (The Noble Heart from Lutetia).

The politician Édouard Herriot, then president of the town council in Lyon, was elevated to the status of *grand cuisinier d'honneur* (honorary grand cook) by the journeyman cooks of the Devoir Unis of that city. The same Union Compagnonnique awarded the historian and senator Justin Godart a scarf of honor in recognition of his book on *compagnonnage* in Lyon, first published in 1909.

To cite another unique example, George Sand was elevated to the rank of honorary *mère* in recognition of her militant support of *compagnonnage* and her related writings. She is the only woman to have been so honored. In addition to her moral and material support of Agricol Perdiguier, in 1841, Sand published a novel entirely devoted to *compagnonnage* with the title *Le Compagnon du tour de France* (The Journeyman of the Tour de France). The journeyman farriers of the *devoir* presented honorary colors to Aurore Sand, granddaughter of the famous novelist, whose memory is commemorated by the annual placement of flowers on her grave in Nohant.

I am very busy with a novel that is more than half finished and that will be read, I hope, a little, on the Tour de France. It is your book that inspired it, and if it contains any poetry or any principles of value, the honor is yours. I count on you to help me with the corrections, for I may have made some mistakes about journeyman customs. I also intend, with your permission, to publish a little article about you and your book. Those who are known as "people of the world" must learn that there are grander ideas and grander sentiments in the workshops than in the salons.

—George Sand, letter to Agricol Perdiguier,
September 20, 1840

The Example of the Stone Masons: Strasbourg

Opposite: **Strasbourg Cathedral**

Right: **Detail of one of the facades of the provincial chapter house of the Association Ouvrière des Compagnons du Devoir du Tour de France in Strasbourg**

STRASBOURG

In the world of *compagnonnage*, the very name Strasbourg evokes many images: the cathedral, its spire, architects Erwin von Steinbach and Jost Dotzinger, the German journeyman's *Bauhütte*, and the cathedral museum. As with Chartres, a stop in Alsace is likely to make journeymen reflect on the cathedral builders and their legacy.

The Example of the Stone Masons of Strasbourg

Between Bishop Wernher, who, in 1015, undertook to build what was initially envisioned as a Romanesque basilica, and Johannes Hultz, who, between 1419 and 1439, constructed the superb pyramidal spire whose tip is some 465 feet above the ground, many designers and workers contributed to the glory of Notre-Dame de Strasbourg. Prominent among them is an architect of genius, Erwin von Steinbach, whose remarkable design (1248–1318) was completed by Ulrich von Ensingen early in the fifteenth century. In the mid-fifteenth century, the cathedral's Gothic forms rose to lofty heights. Thanks to its majestic spire, for many years the tallest in Europe (it was surpassed by the nineteenth-century cast-iron spire of Rouen Cathedral), Strasbourg proclaimed in the skies of Alsace the grandeur of God and the skills of human workers. This prodigious masterpiece brought international renown to the city's builders. Cologne, Vienna, Zurich, and Freiburg set out to follow Strasbourg's example. The stonecutters and masons working on these various projects decided to organize themselves into *Hütten* (lodges) under the authority of the *Hütte* of

Strasbourg, henceforth considered the *haupt-Hütte* (grand lodge). An organization had been born, and known collectively as the *Bauhütte*, this German journeymen's association was rapidly consolidated.

From the Statutes of Ratisbonne to the Imperial Ordinances

In April 1459, master stonecutters from all parts of Germany assembled in Ratisbonne to draft statutes to be honored by all of their *Hütten*. Strasbourg, Vienna, Passau, Landshut, Esslingen, Constance, Cologne, Berne: all the lodges of the *Bauhütte* were represented. Elaboration and codification of the statutes was overseen by the architect of Strasbourg Cathedral, Jost Dotzinger.

The Statutes of Ratisbonne—drafted under the auspices of the Holy Trinity, the Virgin Mary, and the "four crowned ones," patrons and protectors of the stonecutters and the masons—stipulate several moral principles and customs that were to be honored. Earlier traditions of the craft were reconciled in view of "forming a fraternal community, this for the good and utility of all masters and journeymen of the craft guild of stoneworkers and masons on German soil."

The hierarchical organization of the *Bauhütte* is apparent in the designation of four major lodges: Cologne, Vienna, Berne, and Strasbourg, the latter retaining its preeminence as the "mother" city, to use the journeyman lexicon. The Statutes of Ratisbonne were built around major axes such as craft customs, notions of mutual aid and solidarity, and, finally, professional training. Furthermore, they fixed what were henceforth to be the rights of itinerant workers, stipulating the terms under which they were to be welcomed by each *Hütte*. Here we touch upon the core of journeyman philosophy, with its emphasis on travel, on the freedom to move from one worksite to another and from one city to another. A century later, in 1563, the Strasbourg ordinances, also known as the Imperial Ordinances, completed and extended the Statutes of Ratisbonne: "No master, overseer, or journeyman will teach anyone not affiliated with his guild how to make a working drawing."

The ordinances confirm the protection and support that was to be accorded traveling workers. They also prove the existence of passwords, greetings, and signs known only to members of the *Bauhütte*. Fidelity to one's group is declared a sacred obligation, and it is stressed several times that members are to be discreet with nonmembers.

A perusal of the seventy-three articles of the Strasbourg ordinances reveals several similarities with the organizational structure and regulations in force on the journeyman Tour de France. Some authors have suggested that they may constitute the origins of Freemasonry, but this theory has not been proven.

When passing through Strasbourg, Tour-de-France journeymen will certainly remember the stonecutters and the overseers who came before them. The *Bauhütte* entered a period of decline in the early eighteenth century, but it remains a symbol of workers' solidarity dear to journeymen, who see it as an

Opposite: **Simon, *Industrial Parade in Strasbourg*, 1840, Musée des Arts et Traditions Populaires de Paris**

Right: **Stonecutters' assembly room in the cathedral museum, Strasbourg**

expression of the same commitment to spiritual progress and craft training that they themselves feel.

The Cathedral Museum

However enriching, a visit to the cathedral is not sufficient for understanding the period in European history that experienced many great building projects. Thus it is not surprising that journeymen on the Tour de France are among the most assiduous visitors to the cathedral museum, a historical treasure trove that is, in effect, the cathedral's memory bank.

The forty-two rooms of this building, erected from the fourteenth to sixteenth centuries, offer countless opportunities for time travel. Plans and working drawings relating to the cathedral make it possible to appreciate the mastery of the art of drawing possessed by the *magister operis*. Cathedral plans were generally traced with extreme care on pieces of parchment, which were then glued together for sheets of the requisite size. So important were they that the organization responsible for the building's ongoing construction insisted that working drawings be surrendered whenever an architect left the project, including those bearing his own signature.

Journeymen who contemplate these drawings will almost certainly be reminded of cathedral builders from another place and time. Sheets with only passing interest for many visitors are likely to retain the attention of most journeymen.

The cathedral museum in Strasbourg also houses other marvels. From eleventh-century stained-glass windows to chests of the confraternities to a beautiful collection of statues,

the visitor finally arrives in a peculiar room that is the sixteenth-century assembly room of the stonecutters, which survives intact. Here more than anywhere else, journeymen on the Tour de France can envision the daily life of craftsmen of the past. Incontestably, the cathedral museum makes it possible to understand more clearly the universe of the cathedral, which can be better appreciated only after one acknowledges the role of the workers who built it.

Journeymen in Strasbourg

For traveling journeymen, the towns of Alsace hold many attractions: historic walls with watchtowers, beautiful residences with stepped overhangs, carved paneling, and superb *portes cochères* with monogrammed keystones. As in so many parts of France, itinerants are only enriched by their exposure to these remarkably preserved monuments.

The only journeyman organization with a chapter in Strasbourg is the Association Ouvrière des Compagnons du Devoir, with its chapter house situated in a former barracks. On the Tour de France, this chapter house is famous for its heavy metalwork door, fabricated by journeyman blacksmiths-ferriers-mechanics of the *devoir*. Those walking down the street who pass the door will find it nearly impossible to resist touching this work after admiring its beauty. This monumental work in wrought iron was actually designed in Paris, under the direction of *Parisien la Bonne Volonté* (Good Will from Paris). Its fabrication was overseen by *Vanetais l'Ami du Travail* (The Friend of Work from Vanet), with *Briard l'Ami des*

Opposite: **Judgment of Solomon,**
stained-glass window in
Strasbourg Cathedral

Above: **A Chain of Alliance,**
the ceremony after which the
Strasbourg chapter house of
journeymen of the *devoir* is
named

Right: **Spiral staircase in the
cathedral museum**

Far right: **The elaborate metalwork gates of the Strasbourg
chapter house of journeymen of
the *devoir* on rue Wasselonne,
Strasbourg**

Following pages: **Nineteenth-
century print depicting the
departure on the Tour de France**

Compagnons (The Friend of *Compagnons* from Brie), *Armoricain le Persévérance* (The Determined One from Brittany), and *Parisien la Noblesse du Devoir* (The Nobility of the *Devoir* from Paris) who produced various parts of it using medium and large forges and steam-hammers. *Parisien Va de Bon Coeur* (The Good-Hearted One from Paris) and *Île-de-France l'Estimable* (The Estimable One from the Île-de-France) fashioned its mechanical parts—quite tricky, for its unusual weight complicated the task of hinging it. The final assembly was entrusted to *Albigeois la Fermeté* (The Firm One from Albi). With this monumental gate, journeymen displayed their love for fine craftsmanship.

The Chain of Alliance

The symbolic name of the Strasbourg chapter, *À la chaîn d'alliance,* or chain of alliance, is also the name of a ritual ceremony current in all French journeyman organizations. Chains of Alliance are always performed in the same way. After the *rouleur* strikes his staff on the floor three times, the journeymen, all wearing their colors, form a circle in the middle of the room, crossing their arms and taking one another's hands, thereby creating a symbolic chain of which each journeyman constitutes a link. An elder, the *mère,* and the *rouleur* can stand in the middle of this Chain of Alliance. The elder then intones a traditional chant always used in these ceremonies, "The Sons of the Virgin":

In the brilliant art of which Jacquard was grand master
Now it happened that an honest aspirant
Asked himself: When can I learn
The charming secret of the beautiful *devoir?*
Sweet Minerva, ah! Support my effort
To obtain these signal favors.

Then the chorus is sung by all the journeymen in the chain while the circle turns to the right:

For I'd like to be able to weave the chain
That serves to link all hearts.

The general public can witness this appealing ritual, which is usually performed at midnight, during celebrations that are open to the family and friends of participating journeymen. The *gavots* have another name for the Chain of Alliance: the *ronde unitaire,* or round of unity. It is a very beautiful symbol of the fraternity and solidarity that links journeymen on the Tour de France.

The School of the *Indiens*: Romanèche-Thorins

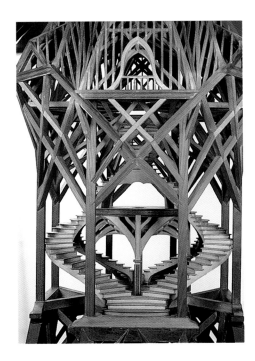

Opposite: **Colors of Pierre François Guillon, known as *Mâconnais l'Enfant du Progrès* (The Child of Progress from Mâcon)**

Above: **Detail of a carpentry "masterpiece"**

Right: **The former school of the *trait* is now a museum of journeyman culture in Romanèche.**

ROMANÈCHE-THORINS

This little village in the department of the Saône-et-Loire, right in the middle of the Beaujolais, some ten miles from Mâcon, is of great interest to anyone intrigued by journeyman traditions. This charming and peaceful town is home to a museum devoted to the glory and achievement of an extraordinary journeyman: Pierre François Guillon, the *indien* of Romanèche. His is a story of the time of workers' universities.

The School of the *Trait*

Born June 13, 1848, in Romanèche-Thorins, Pierre François Guillon completed his Tour de France and became a journeyman carpenter of the *devoir de liberté* on March 19, 1866, in Auxerre, taking as his symbolic name *Mâconnais l'Enfant du Progrès* (The Child of Progress from Mâcon). In 1867, he met Agricol Perdiguier, and the encounter had a profound influence on his humanist orientation. After working in Blois, Paris, Angers, Chenonceaux, and Tours, he returned to Romanèche in 1869 to take over his father's workshop, greatly enriched by his experiences and having acquired formidable skills.

An exceptionally gifted carpenter, Pierre François Guillon took to heart the centuries-old law of *compagnonnage:* pass on the legacy of the elders. In this spirit, in October of 1871, he created the École Pratique de Stéréotomie Appliquée à la Construction (School of Applied Stereotomy). Henceforth, Guillon's reputation spread far and wide. From all the provinces of France as well as from Algeria, Switzerland, and even the United States, students came to Romanèche to learn carpentry, joinery, stair

Above: **Photograph of Guillaume Cartier, known as** *Carcassonne l'Enfant du Progrès* **(The Child of Progress from Carcassonne), one of Pierre François Guillon's best students**

Right: **Guillon with one of his graduating classes**

construction, marquetry, and stonecutting. In his school, he trained a large number of exceptional journeymen, contractors, and stone dressers, including, notably:

J. Boucher, known as *Lamarche le Soutien de Salomon* (The Stay of Solomon from Lamarche), who attended the school from 1874 to 1876. He later became the chief architect of the city of Buenos Aires, Argentina, and the urbanist of Montevideo, Uruguay.

Claude Matrat, known as *Beaujolais l'Enfant du Progrès* (The Child of Progress from the Beaujolais), who attended the school from 1877 to 1879. He built the Palais des Arts Appliqués for the 1925 Exposition des Arts Décoratifs in Paris.

Raoul Thorel, known as *Louviers l'Ami du Trait* (The Friend of the *Trait* from Louviers), who attended the school in 1879 and 1880. He later built the Palais des Eaux et Forêts for the 1900 Exposition Universelle in Paris as well as the Tancarville embankments in Le Havre.

Victor Auclair, known as *Bourbonnais l'Enfant du Progrès* (The Child of Progress from the Bourbonnais). After studying with Guillon from 1883 to 1885, he went to South America, where he helped to rebuild the cities of Valparaiso and Santiago, Chile, after they were severely damaged by earthquakes. Auclair was instrumental in popularizing the use of reinforced concrete, and the cathedral in Santiago is his masterpiece in this technique.

Guillaume Cartier, known as *Carcassonne l'Enfant du Progrès* (The Child of Progress from Carcassonne). After studying with Guillon from 1893 to 1895, he worked on many important projects in France and South America. His specialty was hoisting materials during the construction of aqueducts.

Alexandre Morel, known as *Lyonnais la Loyauté* (The Loyal One from Lyon). Thanks to the training he received at Romanèche, in 1927 he was named one of the first *Meilleurs Ouvriers de France*. He put his talents to use in Morocco, Canada, the United States, Mexico, and Switzerland. Some of his "masterpieces" are on exhibit in the museum.

In addition to being an extraordinary professor of the *trait*, Pierre François Guillon was also mayor of Romanèche-Thorins, a freemasonic dignitary, and president of the superior council of the *devoir de liberté*. He died in 1923, but through the museum in Romanèche, which is housed in his former school, his memory and work remain alive on the Tour de France. All lovers of *compagnonnage* owe it to themselves to visit this sanctuary of the *indiens*, which was founded by the son of Pierre François Guillon, Osiris Guillon, who wanted to assemble in one place the remains of his father's work.

Extracts from the Rules of the School of the *Trait*

"Classes will be attended regularly by the students. All working drawings are to be executed at reduced scale. There will be no exceptions to this rule. Construction using full-scale working drawings will complete this educational method.

"The school accepts as students those at least fifteen years old who have begun their apprenticeships, unless they intend to do so at the school.

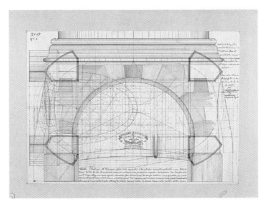

Above: **One of the many working drawings executed at Guillon's school**

Left: **Hieroglyphic carpenter's marks**

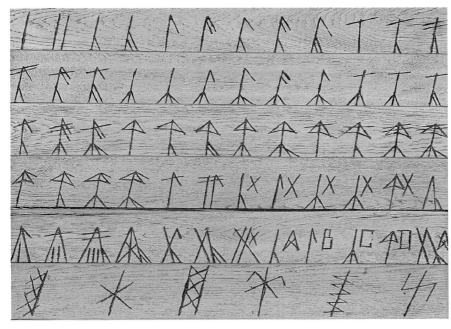

"Students are boarders, the cost of their food and lodging is paid every month. Working hours are as follows: 7:00 to 11:00 A.M., 1:00 to 5:00 P.M., 7:00 to 9:00 P.M.

"At the end of each month, the director sends evaluations of the student's work to his parents, specifying the courses attended and the models executed.

"Students ready to demonstrate a three-year level of professional competence are examined by a departmental committee of technical education in order to obtain a certificate of professional capacity.

"Students also compete for medals and other rewards sponsored at the school by the Ministry of Commerce and Industry, by regional architects' societies, and by other technical organizations."

The *Trait*

This term, specific to the vocabulary of *compagnonnage*, designates a science relative to drawing, or more precisely, a way of representing volumes in depth. An art of stereotomy, the *trait* is also a kind of applied geometry practiced without the abstract formulas required by descriptive geometry. In more concrete terms, the notion of the *trait* encompasses a set of graphic techniques facilitating the production—at reduced scale or full scale, on paper, on parchment, or even on the ground—of working drawings needed to complete structures in wood or stone.

For centuries, youngsters on the Tour de France have been initiated into the mysteries of the *trait* in courses given by jour-

neyman professors who are past masters of its subtleties. In fact, the working drawings used in realizing great "master-pieces" of carpentry are just as remarkable as the artefacts themselves. A visit to the museum in Romanèche-Thorins demonstrates this.

The *trait* transforms the work as well as the worker. With the support and supervision of his professor, the student thinks, reflects, and learns to envision differently. It is in this spirit that we can understand the definition of the *trait* formulated by the journeyman *Aveyronnais la Clef des Coeurs* (The Keystone of Hearts from Aveyron): "The *trait* makes anyone who has mastered it a visionary in spatial depth. It is the alchemy of solids. Numbers are scientific but lines are initiatory." Finally, we note that the art of the *trait* is not restricted to journeyman carpenters, joiners, and stonecutters. Like the tinkers, journeymen in many crafts continue to teach this noble skill so dear to Father Guillon.

The Indiens

In the vocabulary of *compagnonnage, indiens* are none other than journeyman carpenters of the *devoir de liberté*. They themselves have given several accounts of the origins of this nickname. One legend dates it to the period of the construction of the Temple in Jerusalem, maintaining that the journeyman carpenters working for Solomon were placed under the authority of two masters named Perrin and Diem. According to this account, the name derives from a consolidation of the two names: *père indien*, or father *indien*.

Some journeyman carpenters of the *devoir de liberté* read esoteric meaning into the name, India being in their eyes synonymous with the land of ancient tradition. Such is the opinion of Henri Germain, known as *Genevois l'Immortel Souvenir* (The Immortal *Souvenir* of Geneva), for whom "certain high places of the planet are designated by the word 'India,' which signifies sacred ground." Another, more rational account holds that the name derives from the first three letters appearing on the symbolic coat of arms of journeyman carpenters of the *devoir de liberté:* I.N.D. Just as interesting is the hypothesis that the nickname derives from the fact that in the late nineteenth and early twentieth centuries many journeyman carpenters of the *devoir de liberté* worked on projects in South America, which in the past was sometimes confused with the West Indies.

In the end, the mystery of the *indiens* remains unsolved. After the merger of 1945, the last of them entered the ranks of the Fédération Compagnonnique des Métiers du Bâtiment, affiliated with the organization of the journeyman carpenters of the *devoirs* of the Tour de France. A few *indiens* have opted for independence from the FCMB, preferring to maintain their rite in complete autonomy.

Visitors to the Musée Guillon in Romanèche-Thorins will discover just how enamored were the *indiens* of a body of symbolism and legend that ascribed to them a unique role in French *compagnonnage*.

The Children of Osiris

As busy as he was, Pierre François Guillon took the time to write lyrics for several journeyman songs. One of them is especially indicative of the importance to the *indiens* of myth, legend, and symbolism. It occupies a privileged place in the heritage of journeyman carpenters of the *devoir de liberté:*

Wonderstruck by nature
We sing here the memory
Of the gentle, alluring field
Where the learned once lived,
All studiously pursuing science
And working for perfection.
Let us swear allegiance to them
And prove worthy of their tradition.

India the cradle, noble spark
Of the initiated to whom you gave birth,
Distant benefactor,
Bestow upon us a token of the love
You gave us by your noble example.
If we took the name of *loups*
It was to revenge your innocence.
Oh Osiris, protect your children.

Opposite, left: **Journeyman carpenter of the *devoir de liberté*, or *indien*, in ceremonial dress**

Opposite, right: **Detail of the great "masterpiece" of the *indiens***

Right: **Certificate of initiation, featuring a wealth of the journeyman allegories and symbols dear to members of the *devoir de liberté***

In the land of Jerusalem
Where Solomon wanted to build
That gigantic edifice,
The temple that induced clarity,
Apprentices, journeymen, and masters
All worked on Mount Lebanon
And under the aegis of the learned architect
All understood the work "liberty."

From Mount Moria drawing the heights
And tracing the sacred amity,
Beauty supreme, marvel and grandeur,
Secure the glory of the *devoir de liberté*.
If in your breast the triple alliance
Has made us worthy journeymen
We will venerate your birth
And support your name, oh Solomon.

Journeymen who possess the titles
Formerly given to the Holy Science,
Hiram said to follow the doctrine
of the gospel dictated to journeymen
In honor of this great genius
We will gather acacia flowers
Forget not that geometry
Was bequeathed to us by this great founder.

Let us honor this workers' sect
Whose birth was so difficult
We follow in the steps of our ancestors.
Let us imitate them, it is an honor.
They gave to ancient Egypt
Monuments worthy of a great renown
That rightly won them
The beautiful name of *compagnon*.

And then we finish our days
In the heart of a family.
We respect our colors until the tomb,
May they follow us always.
One of our brothers, Guillon, sought to please you
And from him, accept these seven verses.
They were conceived in Romanèche
By the Child of Progress from Mâcon.

The Mother City: Lyon

LYON

Journeymen have always had a special regard for Lyon. An obligatory and celebrated stop on the Tour de France, the capital of the Gauls can take pride in a prestigious past. Even today, Lyon is one of very few cities that is home to chapters of all three French journeyman organizations: the Union Compagnonnique des Devoirs Unis, the Association Ouvrière des Compagnons du Devoir, and the Fédération Compagnonnique des Métiers du Bâtiment.

In July 1988, Lyon had the rare honor of playing host to the eighth assembly of the European journeyman organizations, striking proof of its widespread renown among journeymen.

A Prestigious Past

An entire book would be required to do full justice to Lyon's role in the early history of *compagnon*. The now vanished organization of journeyman dyers of the *devoir* inducted all of their members in this one city, which they considered the "mother" city of their Tour de France. This is just one example of the importance of Lyon to *compagnonnage*.

The so-called city of *canuts* (*cannes nues*, or unadorned staffs) long held a monopoly on the fabrication of journeyman staffs as well as color lithographs and other souvenir images pertaining to Sainte-Baume. It also produced most symbolic journeymen's colors, which is not surprising, given the city's venerable tradition as a center of silk production.

From *L'Illustration*, 1845, reception ceremony for a journeyman carpenter of the *devoir*. His "masterpiece" having passed muster with his judges, the new journeyman swears an oath of allegiance to his *devoir* before the assembled membership.

Journeymen of all rites will remember that Agricol Perdiguier was First Journeyman of Lyon in 1828. Also in Lyon the first step was taken toward creating the future Union Compagnonnique des Devoirs Unis, with the establishment in 1842 of the Fédération des Amis de l'Industrie, which in 1864 became the Société des Compagnons des Devoir Réunis. The first president of the Union Compagnonnique, Lucien Blanc, settled in Lyon, where from 1860 to 1900 he worked as a banker.

The journeyman's Lyon also holds the famous Vaise quarter, which has always been home to the inns and then the chapter houses of many craft organizations. An obligatory tour stop for most of them, Lyon is also the city of journeymen carpenters:

> It was in an August precinct of Lyon
> That I presented myself to the journeymen,
> My heart agitated with fear,
> The fear of being refused.
> Nonetheless, taking courage,
> I was received journeyman carpenter,
> Extracting myself from slavery
> By swearing the oath of fidelity.
>
> —*La Gloire*, eighteenth-century song lyric by
> *Nivernais sans Regret* (Without Regrets from Nevers)

The Competition of Lyon

Early in the nineteenth century, the rival groups of journeyman carpenters known as *soubises* and *indiens* competed for the monopoly of Lyon. To decide who would prevail, they erected a wooden bridge over the Saône River. Each organization was to build half of it, proceeding from opposite banks toward the center. The group whose portion was the better constructed of the two would win the right to practice in the city. According to the story, when the two halves of the bridge met, each party had completed its assigned task with such expertise and precision that they joined perfectly, with no necessary adjustments. The jury of local architects responsible for judging the results had no choice but to declare a draw. Accordingly, it invited the two rival *devoirs* to coexist peacefully in the city.

Confronted with this unexpected outcome, the two groups reconciled with one another, and, after many embraces, handshakes, dances, and songs, agreed to a truce. Unfortunately, this fraternal unity proved short-lived: quarrels and brawls soon erupted between the city's rival camps of journeyman carpenters.

The Association Ouvrière des Compagnons du Devoir du Tour de France in Lyon

It was in Lyon that the first chapter of the Association Ouvrière des Compagnons du Devoir was established. Inaugurated on October 24, 1943, it symbolized the desire to merge the various *devoirs* despite the torments of World War II and the occupation. Thus Lyon became the founding city of

Right: **Regional training center for journeymen of the *devoir* in Lyon, dedicated May 6, 1994**

Below: **Courtyard of the provincial chapter house of the Association Ouvrière des Compagnons du Devoir du Tour de France in Lyon**

the Association Ouvrière. This explains the symbolic name of the Lyon chapter, *Aux Troix Fondateurs* (At the Three Founders), a reference to Solomon, Jacques, and Soubise that was meant to evoke the dream of consolidating the three rites associated with them into a single journeyman family:

> Oh Lyon, city dear
> To all journeymen,
> Yes, in our own regions
> We will sing your name
> And these joyful songs
> Will stir the hearts
> Of a young generation
> Hardened by misfortune.
>
> You will remain an antenna
> To lead our children.
> You had a painful birth,
> Taking a first step.
> One day a sovereign work
> Took shape in you
> That will spread forever
> From city to plain.
>
> If a few malcontents
> In this world
> Reproach in turn
> The spirit of your children,

> The voice of their consciences,
> The journeyman's voice,
> Will later (yes, oh patience)
> Give you vindication.
> —Lyrics by *Pierre le Saintonge* (Pierre from Saintonge), 1948

These lyrics hint at the difficult circumstances surrounding the creation of the Association Ouvrière. Having received its charter from Marshal Pétain, this new organization was variously received by the different journeyman families. The last couplet evokes the break that resulted from this attempt to rejuvenate *compagnonnage* during the occupation.

Since the establishment of its first chapter in Lyon, the Association Ouvrière des Compagnons du Devoir has managed to grow and develop, becoming a powerful movement recognized throughout the world of *compagnonnage*. Now boasting the largest membership of the current French journeymen's organizations, the Association Ouvrière has come a long way since its early, more troubled years.

Thus for journeymen of the *devoir* on the Tour de France, *Aux Trois Fondateurs* is not a chapter like any other. This house in the Vaise quarter has become a symbol and an important point of reference in the history of French *compagnonnage*.

Right: **French and German journeymen are on cordial terms with one another**.

Below: **Progress book of a touring German journeyman**

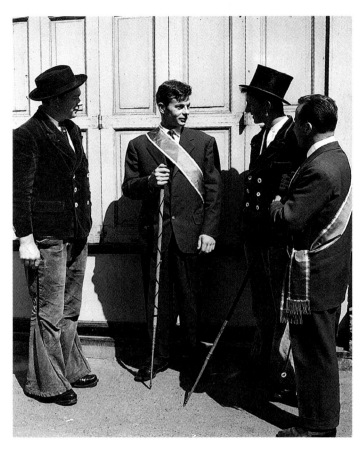

Journeyman Training

For as long as *compagnonnage* has existed, journeymen have received the better part of their training on the Tour de France. Clearly, recent advances in transportation constitute the first great difference between past and present tours, for journeymen no longer travel from stop to stop on foot. A second recent development is that youngsters can now complete their training outside France. Switzerland, Belgium, Germany, Holland, Canada, and the United States regularly play host to young itinerants seeking to learn about new approaches, practices, and techniques relating to their chosen craft. Despite technological innovations and standardization, the tradition of travel continues to play a vital educational role. Without such tradition, there would be no reason for *compagnonnage* to exist in a postindustrial society.

As in the past, traveling journeymen can count on the confidence and goodwill of many patrons. Small-scale employers, who have always respected and sustained *compagnonnage*, have now been joined by directors of medium- and large-scale enterprises who welcome itinerants on the Tour de France as interns. As experienced professionals, sometimes journeymen themselves, these supervisors help aspirants to discover, acquire, and perfect the skills indispensable to their profession. Journeymen's organizations have never placed their young members haphazardly.

At all stops on the Tour de France, young workers find classrooms as well as fully equipped workshops. Teachers and journeymen alike are expected to increase their general and professional knowledge by taking night courses. Whether undergoing an apprenticeship or pursuing more advanced training, the youngsters are given opportunities suited to their particular needs. In the modern era, the augmentation of professional engagements with training provided by the chapter is central to the journeyman's education.

Thanks to this method of training, motivated young men can satisfy the course requirements needed to qualify for government licenses. But make no mistake—*compagnonnage* is not merely a private organization providing professional training. Rather than just a means of professional qualification and certification, journeymen prefer to think of their educational itineraries in terms of advancing along a path of enlightenment, a notion much more in the spirit of the *devoir*. Indeed, in *compagnonnage*, professional competence is inseparable from the personal qualities of the individual. Journeyman education not only addresses manual skills but stimulates the intellect, which is tested throughout the worker's progress. To become a journeymen of the Tour de France, successful presentation of a "masterpiece" does not suffice; the candidate's comportment, his manner of acting in society, is also taken into account. Thus it is best to think of the journeyman's education as an ambitious and generous program intended to make the candidate happy through, with, and in his craft.

Above: **An 1861 lithograph of a journeyman carpenter of the** *devoir*

Right: **A carpentry "masterpiece"**

Below: **An 1861 lithograph of a journeyman dyer of the** *devoir* **wearing his symbolic apron**

The Confédération des Compagnonnages Européens

In July 1988, Lyon was chosen as the site of the eighth assembly of European journeymen's associations (known in French as the Confédération des Compagnonnage Européens and in German as the Europäische Gesellenzunfte). This organization is the result of several attempts to bring German and French journeymen together in the years following World War II.

The confederation was officially inaugurated in August 1953, when it held its first assembly in Luxembourg. France was represented there by the Union Compagnonnique des Devoirs Unis and the Fédération Compagnonnique des Métiers du Bâtiment, the Association Ouvrière having opted not to become affiliated with the new organization. Among other issues, it was decided that assemblies would be held every five years and that other journeyman organizations were welcome to take part in the experiment. UNESCO devised a green-and-white flag for the occasion, colors that have come to symbolize pan-European *compagnonnage*.

The 1958 assembly was held in Hamburg; the third gathering in 1963 was hosted by Copenhagen, an occasion marked by the affiliation of Scandinavian journeyman organizations. In 1968, the assembly met at three sites: Versailles, Châteauroux, and Tours. That year the confederation adopted CEG as its official acronym and was recognized as a nongovernmental organization affiliated with the Council of Europe. Belgium became a member state in 1973, when the gathering was held in Neuchâtel, Switzerland.

In 1978, journeymen from throughout Europe again gathered in Hamburg. Brussels was chosen to host the seventh assembly in 1983, when several German organizations that had previously resisted affiliation joined the ranks. At the same time, the acronym CEG was changed to CCEG.

Thanks to the CCEG, pan-European *compagnonnage* has an institutional base that makes it possible for young members of the eight organizations to cross national borders and still enjoy housing and placement privileges. As might be expected, one of the CCEG's principal objectives is to improve "fraternity among peoples by means of travel and the crafts."

The Memory of Perdiguier: Avignon

Opposite: **Painting by *Parisien La Branche du Compas* (The Arm of the Compass from Paris), mid-nineteenth century. Agricol Perdiguier in the ceremonial garb of a *gavot* dignitary**

Below: **The appearance of journeymen's staffs varies according to their date and the craft and rite of their owner. Such staffs remain one of the main attributes of journeymen on the Tour de France.**

AVIGNON

The departmental seat of the Vaucluse is perhaps best known for its Palace of the Popes. But among journeymen, Avignon's renown comes from a quite different source, an exceptional figure who, in the nineteenth century, did much to reinvigorate journeyman organizations that had long been weakened by internal strife. This esteemed journeyman, Agricol Perdiguier, is better known to his own by his symbolic name, *Avignonnais la Vertu* (The Virtuous One from Avignon). In Avignon, on rue Agricol-Perdiguier, one may pause a moment at the foot of the statue honoring his memory.

Today, only one journeyman organization has a chapter house in the city of the popes. It seems only natural that the organization of the *gavots*, the Fédération Compagnonnique des Métiers des Bâtiments, be represented in the land of *Avignonnais la Vertu*. From there, it is only a short car ride to the village of Morières-lès-Avignon, Perdiguier's birthplace. A plaque on the house where he was born, in the heart of the town, bears witness to the gratitude journeymen feel toward a man who profoundly marked the history of French *compagnonnage*.

Agricol Perdiguier

Born December 3, 1805, in Morières-lès-Avignon, Agricol Perdiguier was taught joinery from a very young age by his father. At age 17, he became affiliated with the journeyman joiners of the *devoir de liberté* in Avignon, and set off on his Tour de France, working in Marseilles, Nîmes, and Montpellier, where he was received as a journeyman in 1824, under the symbolic name *Avignonnais la Vertu*. He then proceeded to Béziers, Bordeaux, Chartres (where he became a

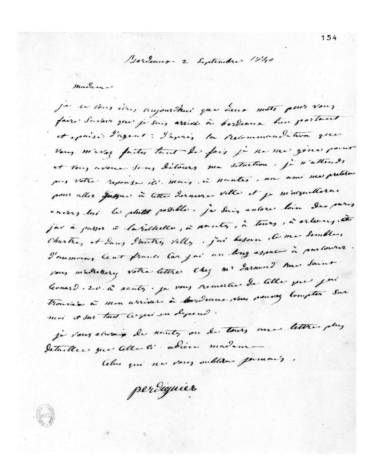

154

"finished" journeyman), Paris, and Lyon. In this last city, his fellow *gavots* made him first journeyman. In 1828, after having completed his stint in this post, he returned to his native village.

During this first Tour de France, Perdiguier was deeply troubled by the incessant rivalries that divided and weakened journeyman organizations. An ambitious and courageous plan to reconcile the three journeyman rites began to take shape in his mind. Henceforth he could no longer remain in Morières.

In 1829, he moved to Paris to improve his mastery of the *trait*, a skill in draftsmanship, taking part the next year in the revolutionary uprisings there. In 1834 and 1836, hoping to foster peace, he published his first journeyman songs. In 1838 he published *"La Rencontre de deux frères"* (The meeting of two brothers), a moving poem in praise of fraternity.

Despite serious health problems, in 1839, he managed to publish *Le Livre du compagnonnage* (The book of *compagnonnage*). It was met with outrage, for this volume was the first to reveal journeyman legends, rituals, and customs to the general public. Furthermore, Perdiguier condemned the absurdity of the quarrels that weakened the *devoirs*. In 1840, to clarify his ideas, he embarked on a second Tour de France. The writer George Sand, who had become a friend after the appearance of the *Livre du compagnonnage*, provided financial support for the project. In 1841, thanks to information provided by Perdiguier, Sand published a novel entirely devoted to *compagnonnage*, *Le Compagnon du tour de France* (The Journeyman on the Tour de France).

Without the help of Sand and her friends, Perdiguier would never have been able to accomplish the mission he had set for himself. For several months, he tried to rally journeymen to his innovative ideas, going so far as to give away copies of his book in cities where he was unable to organize meetings. After his marriage to a young dressmaker, Agricol Perdiguier founded a school of the *trait* in Paris to support his family.

The year 1841 was an important one for Perdiguier. His *Livre du compagnonnage* was published in an inexpensive edition by Laurent Pagnerre. It was very successful, and henceforth among Perdiguier's friends were poets Pierre-Jean Béranger, Alphonse de Lamartine, writers Victor Hugo, Jules Michelet, and playwright-politician Étienne Arago—all of whom, with George Sand, encouraged his project to rejuvenate *compagnonnage*.

After the Revolution of 1848, Perdiguier was elected representative in the Vaucluse as well as in Paris. He opted for the national post and was re-elected in 1849. He was now better placed to make a case for his ideas to a workers' world in need of structural change. But the coup d'état of December 2, 1851, forced him into exile, first in Belgium, then in Switzerland. Struck by illness, *Avignonnais la Vertu* turned this development to account by writing *Mémoires d'un compagnon* (Memoirs of a journeyman).

Once again in France, thanks to the intervention of George Sand, he published another edition of his *Livre du compagnonnage* (1857). In 1863, he set out on a third Tour de France, and this time his ideas were much more warmly

received. Although he was taken seriously, there was still opposition to the project.

The Franco-Prussian War (1870–71) and the tragic episode of the Paris Commune that immediately ensued depressed him. Ill and in debt, he had to sell his property to support his family. With health and financial problems precluding another Tour de France, journeyman organizations began to lose interest in his ideas, which were now considered out of step with reality. On March 26, 1875, Agricol Perdiguier died of a cerebral hemorrhage. He was laid to rest in Père Lachaise cemetery, where journeymen of all organizations now come every All Saints Day to pay him homage.

Nicknamed the Saint Vincent de Paul of *compagnonnage*, *Avignonnais la Vertu* was unable to realize his dream of consolidating the *devoirs* of all rites into a single family united in fraternity. Two lines of verse that he wrote at the end of his life nicely sum up his vision: "May all noble hearts unite / The reign of love is near."

The Frères Pontifes

The confraternity of *frères pontifes* (roughly, "bridge-building brothers") was founded in 1176 by Saint Bénezet, who had set himself the task of building bridges over the principal rivers of southern France. In addition to the famous bridge at Avignon, the brothers worked in Provence, Languedoc, Auvergne, and Poitou. Initially, the community of *frères pontifes* was composed of lay carpenters and stonecutters. Only in 1281 did it become a true religious order.

Bridges often figure as symbols in journeyman iconography, being associated with the *liberté de passer*, or LDP, the right to circulate freely from one place of employ to another, a privilege—at odds with jealously guarded local guild restrictions—granted by medieval kings and lords to workers in the building trades. Many paintings, lithographs, and other journeyman images feature bridges prominently. A few journeymen have even suggested that the *frères pontifes* may have been the originators of *compagnonnage*, but historians have since disproved this claim. Nonetheless, the bridge in Avignon is still greatly esteemed by journeymen on the Tour de France.

The Gavots

Agricol Perdiguier is, without question, the most famous of all *gavots*. But what is the origin of this curious designation, which goes against the general preference among journeymen of assigning men and tools the names of animals, for example *chien*, *loup*, *chèvre*, *renard*, *lapin*, and *pigeon* (dog, wolf, goat, fox, rabbit, and pigeon)?

Before they were known as *gavots*, journeyman joiners and locksmiths of the *devoir de liberté* were known as journeyman *non du devoir*. The term *gavot* came into use only in the early eighteenth century. There are many theories about the word's origin. According to legend, it dates from the schism in Orléans, where some joiners and locksmiths, refusing to accept the new rules imposed by the architects Jacques and Soubise, fled down the Loire River on barges known variously as *gabords*, *gabards*, *gavottes*, or *gavottages*. There is solid historical proof that the *gavots* resulted from a split among journeyman joiners and locksmiths of the *devoir* a few years after the Revocation of the Edict of Nantes (1685), which entailed the separation of Catholic and Protestant journeymen. In this connection, it is worth noting that in southern France, mountain people have long been called *gaves*, *gavouts*, or, on occasion, *gavots*. These designations may owe something to the fact that, after the Revocation, many Protestants hid in the mountains there.

The *gavots* almost disappeared from the landscape of French *compagnonnage*. Only a few dozen remained after World War II. Thanks to the intervention of Pierre Louis

(1906–1986), known as *Limousin Coeur Fidèle* (Faithful Heart from Limousin), however, the organization of journeyman joiners and locksmiths of the *devoir de liberté* was able to reclaim its place and rank on the Tour de France. Pierre Louis, determined to reinvigorate his confraternity, ceaselessly sought out and trained new *gavots*. Thus Louis is a key figure in the pantheon of the *gavots*, second in importance only to Agricol Perdiguier.

Journeyman Staffs

Throughout the world, canes or staffs are associated with pilgrims and wayfarers. Thus journeyman staffs are altogether consistent with Eastern and Western traditions. At a time when roads were unsafe and journeyman organizations were at war with one another, these staffs served above all as weapons. Among journeymen, seizing the staff of one's adversary was long considered a glorious and heroic act. Likewise, losing or, worse, abandoning one's own staff brought shame and dishonor. This is an indication of the degree to which journeyman staffs carried symbolic meanings that transcended their value as functional objects.

Means of physical support, defensive weapons, instruments of measure, and emblems of a certain knowledge, journeyman staffs were the pride of their owners, who received them the evening of their reception. They signified membership in the journeyman confraternity. As in the past, journeyman staffs are now often made of cane. Each one features a metal tip at the bottom and a pommel that, depending on the

Opposite: **From L'Illustration, 1845. When the Tour de France was completed on foot, the way a staff was presented on arriving at the boardinghouse of the _mère_ was a means of identifying oneself.**

Left: **Model of a twisting suspended staircase made by Agricol Perdiguier**

Below: **Model made as a collaborative effort by five journeyman joiners of the _devoir de liberté_, Avignon chapter**

journeyman's rite, is made of ivory, horn, brass, or wood. The latter, most often hexagonal but sometimes octagonal or round, sometimes carries a pastille (brass, silver, or ivory) on which are engraved the journeyman's name, craft, and rite, the city and date of his reception, and a few symbolic letters arrayed around a square and compass or another tool associated with his craft. Finally, all staffs are decorated with two tassels with pompons, their colors varying in accordance with the owner's craft and rite.

The division of the staff into three segments—pommel, main staff, metal tip—is justified by journeyman legend. According to some, the pommel evokes the mallet with which Holem struck Master Hiram, the cane portion symbolizes the ruler wielded by Sterkin against the architect, and the metal tip evokes the crowbar used by another assassin, Hoterfut, to kill him. According to others, the Knights Templar gave staffs to the poor workers who accompanied them to the Middle East.

When one consults journeyman catechisms of the early nineteenth century, the ritual role of the staffs becomes apparent. There were many rules about how it should be held, and some texts from the period describe as many as eighteen ways of carrying it. It was always to be gripped by the right hand, generally with the thumb hiding the pastille. Pointing it tip-end first signified contempt and provocation. Presenting it pommel-end first was a gesture of friendship, peace, and fraternity.

Many situations call for use of the staff. It figures prominently in the ritual greeting known as the _guilbrette_. Even today, when a brother gets married, his fellow journeymen form a vault of staffs over the heads of the couple when they leave the church or town hall. In some organizations, journeymen attending the funeral of one of their own walk behind the hearse carrying their staffs pommel-end down. Journeymen occupying the post of _rouleur_ are provided with a special staff adorned with ribbons so as to be immediately recognized in assemblies. The Association Ouvrière des Compagnons du Devoir du Tour de France has recently begun to provide its young aspirants, at the moment of their adoption, with a short staff lacking a pommel. This is replaced by the traditional symbolic staff on the evening of their reception.

The Lock of the Légion d'Honneur: Marseilles

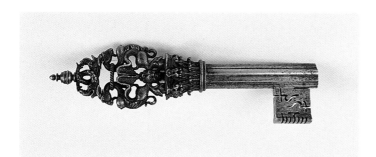

MARSEILLES

Marseilles, Marseilles, unmatched country,
Land of my loves, dear to me always.
Marseilles, Marseilles, hearts brighten,
Dreaming of the Tour, at the thought of seeing you again.
—*La Fraternité de Marseille* (The Fraternity of Marseilles)

In writing these lines, an itinerant stonecutter of the *devoir* paid homage to the special attraction the city, founded by the Phocaean Greeks, had on the Tour de France for centuries, thanks in part to its remarkably sunny climate.

In the past, many journeymen, like the famous joiner François Roux, decided to settle for good in the "unmatched country" of Marseilles. In his *Mémoires d'un compagnon* (Memoirs of a journeyman), Agricol Perdiguier recounts how difficult it was for natives of the region to embark on the Tour de France: "To continue my Tour de France, I had to leave my native land quickly."

To those with an interest in journeyman culture, Marseilles is rich in interesting anecdotes. Aside from being the site of a famous competition between journeyman locksmiths of the two rites in the early nineteenth century, Marseilles is also where journeyman rope makers of the *devoir* first received official recognition. Thanks to the sponsorship of the harness makers, their craft was accepted into the journeyman world in 1735. From archival documents, we also know that in 1777 all journeyman stonecutters of the *devoir* arriving for the first time in the boardinghouse of the local *mère* had their feet

Master locksmiths are capable of superb craftsmanship and precision, as demonstrated by their "masterpieces." Examples can be seen in the Musée du Compagnonnage in Tours, the Musée Calvet in Avignon, and the Musée Bricard de la Serrure in Paris.

Left: **Commemorative print given to journeymen of the *devoir* received in Marseilles**

washed. Journeyman stonecutters have been especially prominent in the history of *compagnonnage* in Marseilles. Indeed, the stone of Provence has long attracted stonecutters of the rite of Solomon and of the *devoir*.

The annals of the journeyman stonecutters are full of symbolic names indicating attachment to Marseilles and Provence. The paternal grandfather of the writer Marcel Pagnol completed his Tour de France as an itinerant journeyman stonecutter of the *devoir* under the symbolic name *La Sincérité de Marseilles* (The Sincerity of Marseilles). In *The Time of Secrets*, the academician recounts how, in 1871, his grandfather was chosen by the journeymen of the Bouches-du-Rhône to go to Paris to restore the belltowers of the Hôtel de Ville, damaged during the tragic events of the Commune.

The Lock of the Légion d'Honneur

In 1807, journeyman locksmiths of the *devoir* and those of the *devoir de liberté* competed for control of the city in a contest of professional skill. It was decided that the organization that produced the most beautiful lock would win a city monopoly good for a hundred years. As their representatives, the *devoirants* chose Ange Bonin, known to his brothers under the symbolic name *Ange le Dauphiné* (Ange from the Dauphiné), while the *gavots* selected one *Provençal le Coeur Content* (The Contented Heart from Provence). On November 30, 1807, each of the competitors was shut up within a secure room, their only access to the outside world being a narrow slot through which food was passed to them. Each journeyman

had at his disposition tools, including a forge, an anvil, a vice, and some hammers. To fashion the lock and key, they were provided with some steel and the fluke of a massive iron anchor. Two journeymen, one from each of the rival organizations, stood guard in front of each room day and night to prevent the competitors from receiving outside assistance.

After eighteen months of confinement, *Ange le Dauphiné* announced that his lock was finished. It resembled a cross of the Légion d'Honneur. The lock casing was adorned with a portrait of Napoleon. One of the three keyholes was shaped like an N. The key was gauged so precisely that upon insertion in the keyhole the escaping air produced a whistling sound, and upon removal there was a sound resembling a soft pistol discharge. Furthermore, the rings of all three keys were masterpieces of engraving. The mechanism, too, was a wondrous thing. *Ange le Dauphiné* had complicated his task by placing inside the lock a chime that rang when anyone tried to force the lock. Determined not to reveal his technical secrets, this exceptional journeyman had also soldered the special tools he had fashioned to complete his work into a magnificent open-work rosette.

After the Lock of the Légion d'Honneur was completed, the *devoirants* chased the *gavots* from Marseilles, for *Provençal le Coeur Content* had not completed his work when his rival presented his "masterpiece." Long in the collection of the Musée Borély, this remarkable object disappeared in 1943. Many suspect it was seized by a Nazi official as war booty. This seems likely, and it may well resurface one day.

Below: **Young man reading aloud the rule of the *devoir* before the assembled members of a journeyman chapter**

Right: **Iron lock from the eighteenth century. Renderings of pediments supported by columns were often incorporated into such locks, for journeymen understood this motif to be a reference to the Temple of Solomon.**

The Chapter House of the Association Ouvrière

The present chapter house of journeymen of the *devoir* was officially dedicated on May 15, 1970. Like all of the organization's venues, this one was given a symbolic name: *À l'étape de Sainte-Baume* (On the route to Sainte-Baume). An apt choice, for pilgrim-*devoirants* on their way to this beloved grotto are given a warm welcome in Marseilles. The house occupies an old mill: as in other cities, the Association Ouvrière has demonstrated considerable intelligence by appropriating an old building and remodeling it to suit its needs.

Like many other such facilities on the Tour de France, the Marseilles house of the journeymen of the *devoir* boasts facilities of various kinds: an apartment for the *mère*, kitchens, dining rooms, a room for the display of "masterpieces," an assembly hall, a library, and workshops.

The Rule of the *Devoir*

In Marseilles, as in all other cities on the Tour de France, newcomers to the Association Ouvrière des Compagnons du Devoir are invited, after the evening meal, to read aloud the organization's rule, or regulatory code. At the designated time, journeymen, aspirants, and workshop enrollees gather in the dining room around an imposing wooden frame, often richly carved. Within it is a sheet bearing text written in a beautiful manuscript hand. When the *rouleur* strikes the floor three times with his beribboned staff, all fall silent and listen attentively as the young man begins to read:

> The journeyman chapter house is a place of reception for apprentices, workshop enrollees, young men from abroad, aspirants, and journeymen traveling in accordance with the centuries-old traditions of journeymen of the *devoir*.
>
> The *mère* or *dame-hôtesse*, journeymen, and aspirants of the various trade organizations guarantee a fraternal welcome to all comers and maintain a like spirit in the daily life of the community.
>
> The rule unites all journeymen. By accepting and observing it, they guarantee that dignity and understanding will reign in their house.
>
> Like a constant invitation to perfecting one's character, the rule functions for all as an educational instrument.
>
> Journeymen, the *mère* or *dame-hôtesse*, the provost, the *rouleur*, and beginning aspirants all play their part in transmitting the journeyman tradition. Honoring the rule that is its

The dream of a journeyman of the
devoir fulfilled at Sainte-Baume,
Musée du Compagnonnage, Tours

Marseilles (with Lyon, Bordeaux, and Paris) was long one of the principal cities of the Tour de France undertaken by journeyman farriers of the *devoir*, as evidenced by this lithograph of 1866, an image celebrating these children of Master Jacques.

issue, they should take care that all members of the community grasp it fully and apply it in exemplary fashion, both within the community and outside of it.

The *rouleur* will have all newcomers read aloud the present excerpts from the rule.

Journeymen, aspirants, workshop enrollees, and apprentices will be acknowledged as *pays* or *coteries* according to their trade or craft.

Customs specific to this community should be adopted gradually by all apprentices and workshop enrollees.

Meals are privileged moments of exchange, special times in the life of the community. When taking one's place at the table, it is customary to greet those already present.

At meals, all persons should be decent, all clothing clean. Napkins are obligatory.

Established mealtimes are to be respected, unless work makes this impossible. All absences and late arrivals should be authorized in advance or cleared after the fact by the provost or the *mère* or *dame-hôtesse*.

Members of the community are not to read at the table, use vulgar language, criticize others when they are absent, quarrel among themselves, or start noisy discussions. They are to avoid staining the table and the floor as well as consuming more than their share of bread and all other food, sharing the meal among one another in fraternal fashion.

At meals and all other manifestations of communal life, everyone's freedom of conscience must be respected and all must avoid imposing their opinions in ways that are unprofessional.

Everyone must pay his monthly bill in advance to guarantee the financial stability of the community.

The rooms are private places of rest and relaxation. Calm should prevail there, out of respect for others.

Access to rooms by all persons foreign to the journeyman chapter house must be authorized by the provost or the *mère* or *dame-hôtesse*.

Apprentices and workshop enrollees who are minors can go out at night only in accordance with the hours established by the provost, to assure they receive the necessary rest.

At work, journeymen, aspirants, workshop enrollees, and apprentices should strive to improve their craft skills. They must respect the personnel and conditions established when they were taken on.

Placement, work absences, and working conditions will be determined by the master of the craft or trade.

In summer as in winter, in exterior workplaces as in workshops within the chapter house, all must wear the traditional dress of their craft so as to ensure safety, guarantee hygiene, and conform with decorum.

The maintenance of workshops, "masterpiece" room, bedrooms, and library is a matter of conscience for each member of the community. Rules are posted in all places where such are deemed appropriate.

Below: **Banner of the Marseilles chapter of journeyman carpenters of the *devoir de liberté***

Right: **The reception pieces of journeyman farriers must demonstrate their mastery of various techniques specific to their craft.**

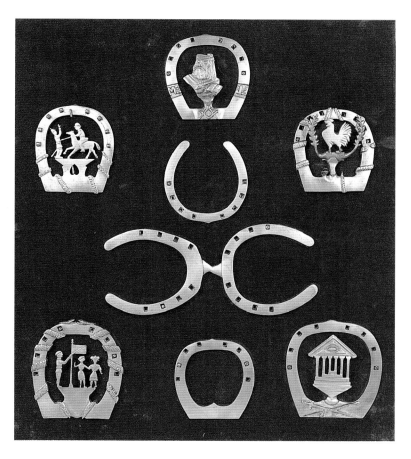

Journeyman life includes many journeyman festivals and manifestations at which members of the community must dress appropriately, in accordance with the traditions of journeymen of the *devoir*. All clothing—jacket, pants, shirt, tie, socks—must be in good condition and very clean.

The present excerpts from the rule constitute, for all members of the community, an engagement of conscience; they are meant to encourage an exemplary attitude, both inside the journeyman chapter house and outside of it.

It is especially incumbent upon journeymen to uphold the spirit of generosity and application embodied in the rule. They must do so with intelligence and firmness, respecting all customary levying of fines and, in serious cases, imposition of disciplinary action.

The rule is the fruit of the experience of journeymen and serves the greater good of the community as a whole.

All apprentices and workshop enrollees invited to live among the journeymen must commit themselves to becoming aspirants and traveling extensively, both in France and abroad, to perfect their professional and cultural knowledge. After which they can be received journeymen of the *devoir*, in accordance with the customs of his trade or craft organization.

After this reading, the newcomer to *compagnonnage* can ask questions prompted by the articles of the rule. Thus the latter provides an official framework for every potential aspirant's first encounter with journeyman institutions. When the *rouleur* again strikes the floor three times with his staff, the ceremony is concluded. All journeymen of the *devoir* of the Tour de France observe this simple ritual.

Journeyman Marks: Nîmes

Above: **The Magne Tower**

Opposite: **The temple of Diana**

NÎMES

𝕋he city of the Gard has always been much frequented by journeymen. Situated between Marseilles and Sainte-Baume to the east and Montpellier and Toulouse to the west, Nîmes is on one of the major axes of the Tour de France. There is no lack of evidence confirming its privileged location, for the many ancient monuments in the department of the Gard still bear countless marks made by journeymen (mostly stonecutters) who come to visit the Pont du Gard, the temple of Diana in Nîmes, the spiral stair at the church of Saint-Gilles, the ramparts at Aigues-Mortes, and the tower in Beaucaire.

From the Temple of Diana
to the Maison Carrée

Parts of the walls of the temple of Diana in Nîmes bear inscriptions, most of them dating from the eighteenth century. Even today, visitors can read symbolic names such as *La Joie d'Orléans* (The Joy of Orléans), *La Réjouissance de Blois* (The Pride of Blois), *La Vertu de Valabrègue* (The Virtue of Valabrègue), *Verdun la Palme de Langre* (Verdun the Victor of Langres), *Joli Coeur de Lion* (Pretty Heart from Lyon), and *Sans Souci de Chignon* (Without a Care from Chignon). Below these names, the journeymen carved the emblem of their craft and its symbolic tools, such as a square, compass, hammer, or edger.

Anyone interested in the traces left in Nîmes by journeymen of earlier periods should also visit the Magne Tower. Although less clear and fewer in number than those on the temple of Diana, a few inscriptions are still visible there, and they hold considerable interest for those fascinated by the world of *compagnonnage*. But journeyman Nîmes is above all represented by the Maison Carrée, whose magnificent doors were made in 1824 by two journeyman joiners of the *devoir*

de liberté. In *Mémoires d'un compagnon*, Agricol Perdiguier recalls: "Maison Carrée . . . is the city's museum. I observed the making of its beautiful walnut entry doors, four inches thick with large copper moldings mortised into the transom and the doors. This work, executed by *Vivarai le Chapiteau* (The Capital from Vivarai) and *Médoc la Rose d'Amour* (The Rose of Love from Médoc), two of our most skillful journeymen, attracted the attention of all the journeymen in our party because of the precision of its workmanship and the beauty of its finish: in terms of execution, it is a masterpiece of joinery."

On Sunday, July 8, 1979, under the auspices of the Union Compagnonnique des Devoirs Unis, the 155th anniversary of the installation of these doors was celebrated. To honor the memory of the two *gavots* who made them, journeymen from Languedoc and Provence installed a bronze plaque commemorating the event on the peristyle of the Maison Carrée.

From the Pont du Gard to the Spiral Stair of Saint-Gilles

Two noteworthy journeyman pilgrimage sites are situated within a few miles of Nîmes. First there is the Pont du Gard, which is visited every year by tens of thousands of tourists. Few of them, however, take the time to observe and appreciate the many marks left by journeymen wishing to pay homage to the builders of the aqueduct, in the process bequeathing their symbolic names to posterity.

All parts of France are represented on the masonry of the Pont du Gard, including several cities whose emblems are carved there: Orléans, Angers, Nevers, Bergerac, Saumur, Vouvray, Libourne, Nîmes, Bordeaux, Paris, Nantes, Bayonne, and Avignon as well as Poitou, Gâtinais, and Saintonge. These geographic indicators appear alongside carvings of squares, compasses, coopers' adzes, rulers, levels, edgers, pickaxes, stonecutters' hammers, and other implements, making it possible to identify each journeyman's craft. Visitors might find it worthwhile to climb to the top level, which boasts many beautiful inscriptions bearing witness to journeymen's admiration for the monument.

These inscriptions are not generic graffiti, much less marks used by the builders, which are found elsewhere on the structure. They are identical to marks found in all the high places of *compagnonnage*. By carving the stone in this way, journeymen paid homage to the genius, both mental and physical, required to erect such a monument. Just as important, they proudly recorded their symbolic names for later generations. By so doing, they became links in a long chain of workers united in their love of fine workmanship. There is nothing ordinary about these inscriptions, for they evidence sustained intellectual and symbolic reflection, broaching the realm of sacred ritual.

The spiral stair in the church of Saint-Gilles-du-Gard is among the places that all journeymen hope to visit one day. The stonecutting is so virtuosic that legend attributes this beautiful work to Brother Mattes of Cluny, said to have been divinely inspired during its execution. Admittedly, those most anxious to see it are journeymen stonecutters, for they alone are able to

Opposite, left: **The doors of the Maison Carrée, made in 1824 by two journeyman joiners of the** *devoir de liberté*

Opposite, top: **The span of Roman aqueduct known as the Pont du Gard is inscribed with many journeyman marks, paying homage to the genius of its builders.**

Opposite, bottom: **Exterior of the Maison Carrée**

Right: **One of the many journeyman signatures engraved in the masonry of the spiral stair of the church of Saint-Gilles-du-Gard**

appreciate fully the incredible spiral vault, whose long arch-stones, with their many curved surfaces, are perfectly joined. Journeyman organizations of all crafts and rites in the Tour de France advise their itinerants to visit Provence and examine the famous structure from the mid-twelfth century.

Immediately upon entering this masterpiece of stereotomy, one encounters engraved marks that continue to the top. *Decharttre le Parisiin* (Decharttre the Parisian), *Joli Coeur de Loudun* (Pretty Heart of Loudun), *L'Espérance le Berrichon* (The Hope of Berrichon), *La Verdure le Picard* (The Verdure of Picardy), and many others engraved sumptuous journeyman emblems that harmonize perfectly with the site, giving it an exceptionally moving dimension. Dozens of later, less elaborate journeyman marks evidence the continuing interest of journeymen.

Brawls and Feuds

Those interested in *compagnonnage* are always surprised by the great contradiction that manifested itself in journeyman organizations from the end of the twelfth century to the first half of the nineteenth century. During this period, rival journeyman organizations cultivated mutual animosity, effectively negating the principle of fraternity that had always been central to the code of the *devoir*. Historians have demonstrated that first religion and then politics were at the root of these sometimes murderous feuds. Agricol Perdiguier deserves great credit for being the first to preach reconciliation to these rival organizations, and this at a time when they sought only to humiliate each other. The work of Perdiguier was long and difficult, and, despite many subsequent attempts at reconciliation and revitalization conceived along similar lines, his dream has remained unfulfilled.

In the eighteenth and nineteenth centuries, Nîmes was often a theater of confrontation between the members of rival organizations, and the results could be bloody. The nearby Crau plain, between the main arm of the Rhône delta and the Alpilles, acquired a dark notoriety in 1730, when it was the site of a ferocious battle between the adherents of enemy journeyman rites. Frédéric Mistral immortalized the event by recounting it in *Calendal*, whose eighth "chant," or song, is devoted exclusively to it:

> The combatants in the mêlée
> Armed with metal-tipped staffs

Above and right: **Journeyman marks carved into the masonry of the temple of Diana in Nîmes**

Opposite: **The Nîmes chapter house of the Association Ouvrière des Compagnons du Devoir, housed in an ingeniously remodeled lime kiln**

Large iron compasses and assassins' tools
Massacred one another. Cried one:
I must open and eviscerate
All the *loups.* Cried another: I must
Cover the ground with the skins of the *chiens.*

All *gavots* to the executioner! Oh cowardly
Race of *loups!* Ah birds of prey,
Pay us, they screamed, for the blood of Hiram.
Bah *loups-garous* and *chiens!* Bah cowards!
Plant our colors, common laborers.
If not, they snarled, we'll make
Grass snakes of you! Forward against the *devoirants!*
And the two groups tore each other's guts out.
Frenzy consumes them, blinds them:
Implacable, they stab each other with compasses
And die, frothing at the mouth.
Caught up in their hard and heady fight
The warriors do not see
That the country is in tears.

Unfortunately, the Crau plain was not a unique example. In 1618, *loups* and *loups-garous* had a brutal encounter in Lunel. The fight was so violent that several journeymen lost their lives. In 1839, three brigades of gendarmes saved the lives of 26 *gavots* who had been attacked by 150 *devoirants* on the railroad line running from Alès to Beaucaire, near Nîmes. In

1840, a brawl in the town of Uzès between a journeyman carpenter and a journeyman cobbler resulted in the latter's death. During this sad period, Provence was one of the most dangerous regions on the Tour de France.

Compagnonnage Today

Between World Wars I and II, there were only two official chapter houses in Nîmes: the journeyman farriers of the *devoir* and the journeyman bakers. As everywhere in France, *compagnonnage* was at a low point during this period. Aspiring journeymen became scarcer due to profound upheavals in the artisanal and industrial worlds.

After World War II, *compagnonnage* in Nîmes showed signs of rebirth. A few journeymen sought to reconfigure the movement's institutions in a way more consistent with its ideals. This handful of people secretly hoped to revive local chapters that had flourished there in the past. As a result of several years' work, two or three French journeyman organizations now have a presence in Nîmes.

The official dedication and lighting of the fires of the Nîmes chapter of the Union Compagnonnique des Devoirs Unis took place on June 11, 1972, marking the realization of the dream of Jean Lavillionière, known as *Berrichon l'Ami du Travail* (The Friend of Work from Berrichon), a journeyman pastry chef who, on the same occasion, was pronounced a "finished" journeyman. Since June 1991, the Nîmes chapter has been housed in a medieval shop in the old city, which donated

the building to the organization on the understanding that the organization would restore it.

The Association Ouvrière des Compagnons du Devoir du Tour de France officially dedicated its chapter house on June 22, 1973, in the presence of Georges Gorse, then the minister of labor. Housed in a former lime kiln, it is the result of many years of restoration work in a quarter that is now part of the ZUP, a prioritized area for urban development, in Nîmes.

The Fédération Compagnonnique des Métiers du Bâtiment preferred to place its local chapter house in Avignon, in the country of Agricol Perdiguier. Thus journeyman culture continues to thrive in Nîmes, which has again become a stop on the Tour de France for several crafts. Both the Union Compagnonnique and the Association Ouvrière strive to make their organizations better known, taking part in many exhibitions and organizing open houses so as to reach a larger public.

We know that during their Tour de France, journeymen, especially stonecutters, made a point of visiting the ancient monuments in our region: the Pont du Gard, the temple of Diana, the spiral stair of Saint-Gilles-du-Gard, the ramparts at Aigues-Mortes, the antiquities of Saint-Rémy-de-Provence, the tower in Beaucaire, the Saint-André stronghold in Villeneuve-lès-Avignon. Many of the inscriptions they left behind are illegible. Several of these marks feature public journeyman emblems: squares and compasses, and also cobblers' hammers. One also sees joiners' hammers and jointing-planes, planers' adzes, harness makers' knives, as well as completed objects such as horseshoes for farriers and bells for founders. These marks are quite eloquent. They indicate the importance of the movement that brought into our region workers from all corners of France.

—Paul Marcelin, *Les Compagnons du Tour de France à Nîmes,* 1963

Competition by Pulpit: Montpellier

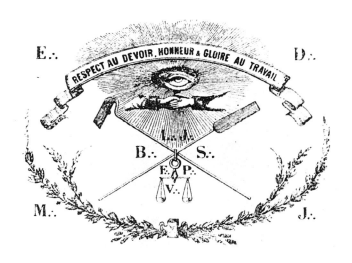

Above: **The symbolic emblem of the journeyman bakers of the *devoir*, children of Master Jacques (EDMI)**

Opposite: **From *L'Illustration*, 1845, a depiction of the welcoming rite performed by journeyman communities for newcomers**

Montpellier, in the department of the Hérault, has always occupied a special place in the history of *compagnonnage*. Although many journeyman organizations once kept chapter houses there, at present, only the Union Compagnonnique maintains a venue in the city. But the regional capital of Languedoc-Roussillon still has a special allure for journeymen on the Tour de France.

The Appearance of *"Syndicat"*

Some historians of the workers' movement have been too quick to forget that the origins of *syndicats*, or trade unions, are found in *compagnonnage*. The very word *"syndicat"* was coined in Montpellier in the first decades of the eighteenth century. Its earliest appearance dates from May 11, 1730, when the city's mayor, Armand François de Lacroix, used it in an ordinance to characterize the disruptive activities of certain journeymen:

> Since time immemorial, journeyman joiners and carpenters, some "of the *devoir*" and others "*gavots*," have fought continuously with one another in ways that have produced countless disturbances. They gather and walk down the main streets, attacking those not of their own party with the staffs with a squared shaft, which they all carry. . . . Driven by unparalleled rage and fury, they fight with one another, sometimes to the point of inflicting death. . . . Fostering still greater disorder, they have undertaken, against the law, to form *syndicats* among themselves and even to deliberate against the bodies of master joiners and carpenters, prohibiting certain journeymen from working in certain workshops. . . . So here we have some of them syndicated against the others and all of them against the masters.

While this ordinance is quite important because of its early use of the term *"syndicat,"* its damning characterization of certain contemporary journeyman practices is also noteworthy. For more than two centuries, Montpellier, like most other cities of the day, experienced brawls between rival organizations, many of them, as the mayor claims, resulting in death.

Furthermore, the *interdit de boutique*, a very efficient weapon, was used often in Montpellier. This practice consisted of "boycotting" a workshop or enterprise, which is to say preventing all workers—journeymen and nonjourneymen alike—from working for employers who refused to grant demands, such as salary increases and improved working conditions, made by their journeymen employees. As a general rule, *interdits de boutique* made it possible for journeymen to obtain satisfaction when their demands were reasonable. There are many examples in the history of *compagnonnage* of journeymen emerging victorious from these struggles with the guild masters.

Montpellier and the *Gavots*

The ordinance of 1730 already attests to the presence of journeyman joiners and carpenters of the *devoir de liberté*, better known on the Tour de France by the nickname *gavots*. The most famous of them, Agricol Perdiguier, was received a journeyman carpenter of the *devoir de liberté* by the Montpellier chapter, one of the most highly regarded on the Tour de France. His reception ceremony took place on All Saints Day in 1824. Thus it was in Montpellier that Perdiguier was first called by his symbolic name, *Avignonnais la Vertu* (The Virtuous One from Avignon).

In his memoirs, Perdiguier devotes several lines to Montpellier, which he clearly found especially attractive: "Montpellier is one of the most agreeable of cities. It boasts the esplanade, the citadel, several handsome buildings, a multitude of beautiful fountains, and, especially, the Place Peyrou, with its remarkable aqueduct, its belvedere, its broad promenades, and its elevated site, from which one's gaze can play over plains, lakes, mountains, and the sea, all leading up to the most vast, most beautiful horizon imaginable."

The Pulpit Competition

The journeyman joiners of the *devoir de liberté* had long disputed with the journeyman joiners of the *devoir* the right to a monopoly in the city. As in Lyon and Marseilles, the rival organizations decided to settle the matter through a "masterpiece" competition, judging this noble approach preferable to the ongoing strife, which was compromising the public image of all journeymen.

The competition took place in 1803–4. To settle the differences between *gavots* and *devoirants*, an independent jury of nonjourneymen proposed that each organization designate representatives to make a pulpit. Whoever produced the most successful "masterpiece" would win the city for his organization, and the losers would leave Montpellier as quickly as possible, not to return for a hundred years. The stakes, then, were high, with each organization placing its prestige on the line.

Understandably, all eyes on the Tour de France were turned toward Montpellier for the duration of the competition.

The *gavots* designated two representatives, *Dauphiné le Républicain* (The Republican from Dauphiné), responsible for the *trait*, or design, and *Percheron le Chapiteau* (The Capital from Percheron), charged with its execution. The journeymen of the *devoir* placed their hopes in one *Nanquette le Liégeois* (Nanquette from Liège), a skillful joiner whose gifts were widely acknowledged.

After many months' labor, the two works were presented to the jury. It was particularly impressed by the beauty of the pulpit made by the *gavots*. The verdict seemed to be in favor of the *devoir de liberté*. But *Nanquette le Liégeois* suggested that the jury ask each competitor to disassemble their "masterpiece." The assembled company was surprised to see the *devoirant* take apart and reassemble his work very quickly, something that the *gavot* could not do. Now the journeyman joiners of the *devoir* claimed victory. But the *gavots* protested vigorously, for the initial verdict of the jury had been in their favor. The outcome was total confusion, as each party claimed victory before a jury unable to reach a final decision. At the end of the competition, *gavots* and *devoirants* were even more irritated with one another than they had been before.

Unfortunately, the pulpit of the *devoirants* was destroyed in a fire in the workshop of the journeyman entrusted with its safekeeping, but a portion of the pulpit of the *gavots* is currently on view in the Museum of Compagnonnage in Tours.

The Journeyman Millennium

Such was the name given to a grand celebration that, it was hoped, would bring the three French journeyman rites together in Marseilles. Conceived by the *pays* Coulet, a journeyman joiner of the *devoir*, its centerpiece was to be a large exhibition of "masterpieces" from throughout France. It was to be accompanied by evening gatherings showcasing journeyman poets and singers, intended to give the event a cultural dimension. The organizers even considered inviting Frédéric Mistral to preside over the celebration's opening ceremonies.

The Journeyman Millennium project was a sign of the growing desire among journeymen, who were feeling weakened by internal quarrels and disoriented by the industrial revolution, to reinvigorate their culture and institutions. Unfortunately, despite its importance as a means of altering public perceptions of *compagnonnage*, the plan fell victim to the prevailing dissensions between rival organizations. The young Union Compagnonnique was not taken seriously by the older *devoirs*. Verbal blunders and personal differences soon stifled this noble enterprise.

In 1907, Montpellier played host to a modest gathering of journeymen that had nothing in common with the original project. Frédéric Mistral disassociated himself from the occasion, which was marked by discord. The crisis then confronting vintners throughout southern France further darkened the atmosphere of this journeyman assembly.

Above: **Commemorative escutcheon of the 1981 Congress of the Union Compagnonnique, held in Montpellier**

Right: **Souvenir Tour-de-France print, 1860**

The *Cayenne* of the Union Compagnonnique des Devoirs Unis

When the Union Compagnonnique inaugurates a new *cayenne*, or local chapter, on the Tour de France, this solemn ceremony is known as the *allumage des feux*, or "lighting of the fires." The *allumage des feux* of the Montpellier *cayenne* took place on March 20–21, 1976, under the aegis of the président général of the Union Compagnonnique at the time, the *pays* André Madrolle, known as *Berry le Décidé* (The Determined One from Berry). Twenty chapters on the Tour de France sent representatives to this two-day gathering, which was of considerable importance for journeyman culture in Languedoc. On Saturday, March 20, sixty-two journeymen attended the ritual *allumage des feux* at the chapter house. At the time, the *pays* Jacques Rolando was president of the organization's Montpellier chapter. The following day, many distinguished figures gathered with the journeymen to celebrate the occasion. Aside from the mayor of Montpellier and representatives of various local business and craft organizations, some fifteen journeymen from the Fédération Compagnonnique des Métiers du Bâtiment were also present, evidence of the friendly relations between these two organizations. A journeyman from the Association Ouvrière des Compagnons du Devoir du Tour de France was also present, giving the event an ecumenical dimension.

Years have passed since those two days in 1976, and the Union Compagnonnique des Devoirs Unis has finally established a true chapter house. This means that the *cayenne* can now receive new members and have regular admission and reception ceremonies. From time to time, the journeyman chapter members organize exhibitions and other events to make themselves better known to the public. They even hold conferences with the Montpellier and Perpignan lodges of the Grand Orient de France, for the Union Compagnonnique has never shied away from official contact with local Masonic organizations. Finally, the Montpellier *cayenne* also maintains close ties with the chapters in nearby Lourmarin and Nîmes.

Rules for Itinerants

1. Arrival

On arrival, the itinerant will introduce himself to the president or other person in authority in the city and give him his booklet. He will then introduce himself to the *mère* or *dame-hôtesse*. The person in authority will accompany him to his employer. Throughout his Tour de France, the itinerant will remain in contact with the godfather in his city of departure.

2. Sojourn

Proper conduct and the highest respect for the *mère* are obligatory. The itinerant should have as much contact with the journeymen as possible, as frequently as possible. Itinerants are to keep the rooms and materials made available to them clean. Each individual will respect others' need for sleep. Proper dress and good bodily hygiene are obligatory. All insulting remarks and vulgar language are prohibited. Conversations about politics and religion are forbidden within the *cayenne*. Active participation in the life of the *cayenne* and attendance at

celebrations is obligatory. Persons unaffiliated with the organization will have no access to itinerants' rooms. Itinerants will obey the rules specific to each *cayenne*. They will keep their payments current.

3. Work

For the sake of the organization's reputation, all itinerants will work conscientiously and with perseverance. Employers cannot be changed without the authorization of the first *pays* of the city or of the president *pays*. The travel booklet must be stamped by every employer.

4. Course Work

All itinerants are expected to attend whatever courses are assigned them by the section. Their goal will be to master their craft perfectly. Likewise, they will learn about *compagnonnage*, its legends, its history, and other journeyman organizations.

5. Departure

The itinerant cannot leave a city until his affairs there are in order. His booklet must have been signed by the *pays* serving as *rouleur*, by the *premier en ville*, and by the president. Before departing, he must bid farewell to the *mère* or *dame-hôtesse*. Like the president, he will inform the commissioner of the Tour de France of his change of venue.

Like the other two French journeyman organizations, the Union Compagnonnique des Devoirs Unis is predicated on respect for a set of rules that governs the behavior of all aspirants and journeymen on the Tour de France. The existence of such rules and regulations determines the quality of any journeyman organization. Thus it would be impossible to exaggerate the importance of these codes for anyone with more than a passing interest in journeyman life and culture. All serious historians of the subject must familiarize themselves with as many such codes as possible.

From the oldest to the most recent, the rules possess qualities of simplicity and grandeur that are at the heart of *compagnonnage*. Rather than relying on long and convoluted explanations, journeymen prefer to sum up its central message in a single word: *devoir*, which signifies profound duty or obligation.

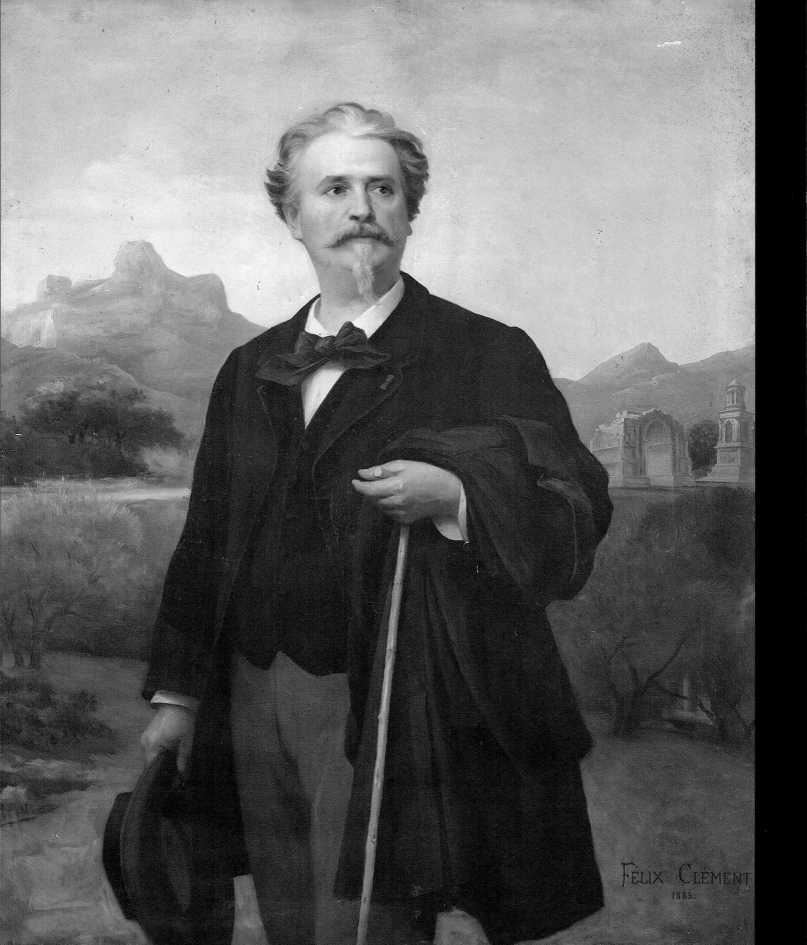

FÉLIX CLÉMENT
1885.

The Frog of Saint-Paul: Narbonne

Opposite: **Portrait of Frédéric Mistral by Clément. This winner of the Nobel Prize for literature was very interested in *compagnonnage*, which figures in several of his writings.**

Above and right: **The famous frog of Narbonne in the holy-water basin in the church of Saint-Paul owes its renown in large part to Frédéric Mistral.**

NARBONNE

Narbonne has never been a major city of the *devoir* on the Tour de France. It was primarily a city one passed through on the way from one place to another. Toulouse to the west and Béziers to the east were considered more important. However, the capital of the Septimanie was the site of events of some significance in journeyman history. In 1785, a few journeymen joiners of the *devoir* from the city sold their fraternal secrets to some linen weavers who wanted to become journeymen. This affair became notorious throughout the Tour de France. After hearing about the episode, the journeyman stonecutters and carpenters of the *devoir* in Bordeaux excommunicated the journeyman joiners of the *devoir* in Narbonne for a period of twenty-five years. Despite the scandal, journeyman linen weavers were henceforth recognized throughout the Tour de France as authentic journeymen.

The various crises that struck vintners in the Narbonnais contributed greatly to the gradual closing of the department's few local journeyman chapters. In the second half of the nineteenth century, Narbonne lost its status as a city of the *devoir*.

The "Drawings" of Saint-Just

Like every city that boasts a cathedral, Narbonne has always attracted journeyman carpenters, stonecutters, joiners, locksmiths, and stained-glass makers eager to admire these majes-

tic structures, in this case the cathedral of Saint-Just.

Like the analogous buildings in Limoges and Clermont-Ferrand, the cathedral of Saint-Just in Narbonne is one of very few French cathedrals for which a few "working drawings" are engraved in stone and survive on the building's exterior, precious reminders of a time when architects produced such images at full scale, sometimes on the ground, to guide their workmen. Admittedly, the examples in Narbonne have been much damaged by erosion. But even today, journeymen who come across them on the terrace outside the building's choir are likely to be moved by these "drawings," traces of a moment still regarded by many as the golden age of *compagnonnage*.

The Frog of Narbonne

Narbonne is best known to journeymen for a famous *remarque:* a frog carved into the holy-water basin shaped like a scallop shell in the church of Saint-Paul. A means of confirming that itinerants on the Tour had indeed been where they said they had, *remarques* were idiosyncratic objects of interest that journeyman-visitors would subsequently be asked to describe. At a time when photography did not yet exist, this was a very efficient test of a journeyman's veracity. If he had indeed visited the town in question, an accurate description of its designated *remarque* posed no problem for him.

The frog of Narbonne owes its considerable fame on the Tour de France to Frédéric Mistral, who immortalized it in *Mes origines, mémoires et récits* (My origins: recollections and stories):

One afternoon in June, comrade Pignolet, a journeyman joiner known as *La Fleur de Grasse* (The Flower of Grasse), was returning full of excitement from his Tour de France. It was sleepy-hot, and, with his beribboned staff in hand and a canvas sack containing his set of tools (chisels, planes, mallets) on his back, Pignolet headed up the wide road leading to Grasse, whence he had departed three or four years earlier.

As was customary for journeymen of the *devoir,* he had just visited Sainte-Baume to pay homage at the tomb of Master Jacques, the father of journeymen, whence, after having engraved his nickname on a rock, he had gone down as far as Saint-Maximin to earn his colors under Master Fabre, the blacksmith who blesses children of the *devoir.* Proud as Caesar, his kerchief around his neck, a jumble of multicolored favors in his hat, two small gold compasses hanging from his ears, he made his dust-covered gaiters crack as he moved. He was solid white.

What heat! From time to time, he looked at the fig trees to see if there were any figs; but they were not yet ripe, and, in the dry grass, green lizards gaped and mad cicadas were on the dusty olive trees. The thorny shrubs and holm-oaks sang in the sun as if possessed.

"God, it's hot!" Pignolet repeated.

He had long since consumed all the brandy in his flask and, gasping from thirst, his shirt was drenched.

"But," he said, "onward! We'll soon be in Grasse! For goodness sake, what happiness, what joy to embrace father and mother and drink jugs of water from the fountains in Grasse, and recount my Tour de France, and kiss Maïon on her fresh cheeks and marry

Opposite: **The cathedral of Saint-Just in Narbonne**

Left: **An apprentice stonecutter with a journeyman, an example of the art of transmitting a craft through word and demonstration**

her at the Sainte-Madeleine, and never again leave the house, the country! Courage, Pignolet, it's not far now."

He had reached the gate of Grasse and, after a few more strides, arrived at his father's shop.

"My lad! Oh my handsome lad!" cried old Pignol leaving his bench. "Welcome! Marguerite, the little one! Run, get some wine, light the fire, lay the tablecloth . . . Oh! What a blessing! How are you?"

"Not too poorly, thank God. And you, here, you're all doing well, father?"

"Ah! Like poor old people . . . But look how he's grown!"

And they all embraced him, father, mother, neighbors, and friends and young girls and children handled the beautiful ribbons on his hat and his long staff; old Marguerite, her eyes full of tears, quickly lit the fire with a handful of wood chips, and while she coated some pieces of dried cod with flour to regale her son, master Pignol and Pignolet sat down at the table and toasted each another's health.

"Well, now," said old Pignol striking the table, "you've completed your Tour de France in less than four years, and you're back already, having become, you say, a journeyman of the *devoir*. How things have changed! In my day, it took us seven years to earn our colors! It's true, my child, that here, in the shop, I gave you a good start, and that, as apprentices go, I admit it, you picked up the plane rather quickly. . . . But in the end, all that matters is that you know your craft and that, apparently, you've seen and learned everything that a master's son should."

"Oh! Father, as to that," answered the young man, "I don't mean to boast, but when it comes to joinery, I don't think anyone can get the better of me."

"Well!" said the old man. "Let's see! While the codfish is crackling in the pan, tell me a bit about the beautiful things you encountered during your travels."

"First off, Father, you know that when I left Grasse, I headed for Toulon, when I worked in the arsenal; no need for me to tell you about what's there; you saw it all long before I did."

"Yes, I know about that, let's move on."

"After leaving Toulon, I got a job in Marseilles; a very beautiful city, you know, with a good job market, where colleagues made sure I took note, Father, of a horse that serves as the sign of an inn."

"Good."

"From there, my faith, I headed up to Aix, where I admired the carvings on the doors of the church of the Saint-Sauveur."

"We've seen all that."

"From there we went to Arles, where we saw the vault of the Hôtel de Ville."

"Put together so well that one can't imagine how it remains standing."

"From Arles, Father, we set off for the town of Saint-Gilles, and there we saw the famous spiral stair. . . ."

"Yes, marvelous in its design and its execution, demonstrating that there were good workers yesterday as there are today."

"Then we headed for Montpellier, and there we were shown the famous 'scallop shell' . . ."

Above: **A journeyman emblem near Carcassonne**

Left: **Auguste Lemoine, watercolor of a *conduite*, or ritual departure procession, 1839**

"Which is in Vignola and that the book calls 'the fan vault of Montpellier.'"

"Exactly. . . . After which we walked to Narbonne."

"This is what I was waiting for. . . ."

"What, Father? In Narbonne, I saw the archbishop's palace and the paneling in the cathedral of Saint-Paul. . . . And then . . . the journeyman song doesn't have much more to say about it:

>   Carcassonne and Narbonne
>   Are two good cities
>   On the way to Béziers
>   Pézenas is nice
>   But the prettiest girls
>   Can be seen in Montpellier."

"Why you little slacker, didn't you see the frog?"

"What frog?"

"The frog in the holy-water basin in the church of Saint-Paul! Ah! I'm not surprised you finished your Tour de France so fast . . . the frog of Narbonne! The masterpiece of masterpieces that people come from all over the world to see! You faker!" cried the old Pignol, becoming increasingly agitated. "You're like a cricket, you jump around so fast! Who says he's a journeyman but hasn't seen the frog of Narbonne! Oh! Let it not be said, my pretty, that a master's son makes him lower his head in our house. . . . Eat, drink, get some rest, but tomorrow morning, if you want us to be friends, my boy, you'll go back to Narbonne to see the frog."

Poor Pignolet, who knew how stubborn his papa could be when he took a notion into his head and that he was by no means joking, ate, drank, went to bed; and the next day, without uttering another word, after filling his sack with provisions, he set out once more at dawn for Narbonne.

His feet bruised and swollen in the heat, thirsty, here he was treading roads and highways again! After seven or eight days, having finally reached Narbonne, poor Pignolet, who this time, I must tell you, was not singing and took no time to eat or drink from the first available bottle, headed right for the church of Saint-Paul and went directly to its holy-water stoup . . . and saw the frog. At the bottom of the marble basin, in effect, under the clear water, a frog with red stripes, carved with such skill you would have sworn it was alive, crouched and looked up, with his gold eyes and cunning snout, at the poor Pignolet come from Grasse to see him.

"Ah! Little toad!" the joiner suddenly screamed wildly. "So you're the one who made me walk two hundred miles in this killing sun! Well then, you won't forget Pignolet from Grasse, known as *Pignolet la Fleur de Grasse!*"

With that, the scoundrel took a hammer and chisel from his bag and wham! With a single blow he sent the frog flying. . . . The holy water, it is said, suddenly turned blood-red. . . . And that was the end of the little frog of Narbonne.

With this story of the famous frog of Narbonne, Frédéric Mistral demonstrated his familiarity with the customs of the Tour de France. But it is worth noting a gross blunder result-

Left: **In *compagnonnage*, professional training consists of a mixture of outside employment and supervised workshops in the chapter house.**

Below: **Coded *Lettre de course*, or journeyman passport, from the 1850s**

ing from his not being a journeyman himself. The symbolic name *La Fleur de Grasse* (The Flower of Grasse) is that of a journeyman stonecutter, not that of a journeyman joiner.

A few years ago, the aunt of a journeyman carpenter of the *devoirs* from the Toulouse chapter, having learned that her nephew would be making a stop in Toulouse but unsure of the precise date of his arrival, left an envelope bearing his name near the holy-water basin in the church of Saint-Paul. She was sure that her nephew would come to "remark" the frog. And indeed, the young man came and found the message that she had left there for him. This is a beautiful story of the continuing tradition of journeyman *remarques*.

Like Narbonne, every city still possesses its own obligatory journeyman *remarques*. It is up to the local elders to point them out to young itinerants during their sojourns.

The City of Carpenters: Toulouse

TOULOUSE

Toulouse, the "pink city," was and remains a capital of *compagnonnage*. Admittedly, the journeymen of Toulouse of today differs markedly from that of yesterday, as the famous chapter house of the *soubises* journeyman carpenters has now become a museum run by the Fédération Compagnonnique. The Association Ouvrière des Compagnons du Devoir has a *prévôté*, or subsidiary chapter house, while the Fédération Compagnonnique has set up shop in a different quarter, building its headquarters and establishing training workshops only a few feet away. The journeymen of Toulouse have also developed solid ties with the neighboring city of Colomiers (where the journeymen of the *devoir* even have a *prévôté*), and with Revel, roughly thirty-seven miles away, which has become an important center of French cabinetry. These introductory remarks about the Toulouse beloved of carpenters would be incomplete if we failed to mention Aimé Liabastres, known as *Auvergnat l'Ami du Trait* (The Friend of the *Trait* from Auvergne), dubbed by Raoul Vergez the "guardian of the traditions" of *compagnonnage*.

Above: **From *L'Illustration*, 1845, two journeyman carpenters, a *rouleur* and an employed itinerant**

Right: **Certificate of thanks of an itinerant journeyman carpenter of the *devoir*, *bon drille* of Father Soubise**

Opposite: **Print in gouache with additions in ink, Musée Dupuy, Toulouse. Reception diploma of an itinerant journeyman carpenter of the *devoir*, *bon drille* of Father Soubise**

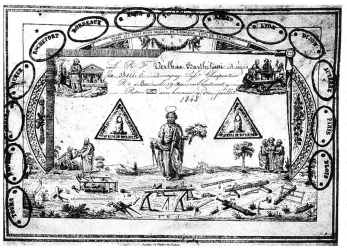

Above: **Bracelet of a *mère* of the Association Ouvrière des Compagnons du Devoir du Tour de France**

Right: **From *L'Illustration*, 1845, procession of journeyman carpenters on Saint Joseph's Day**

Saint Joseph's Day

Journeyman culture in Toulouse has always been dominated by the *soubises*. The museum in their former *cayenne* (as they call their chapter houses) serves as a permanent reminder of their centuries-long presence in the city. Every year on March 19, Saint Joseph's Day, in accordance with a long-standing tradition, the journeyman carpenters of the *devoirs* of the Fédération Compagnonnique march in solemn procession through the center of Toulouse. This appealing and impressive procession is led by the *rouleur* and accompanied by fanfares. Several "masterpieces," those of newly received journeymen as well as older ones thought to be especially prestigious, are carried by young itinerants, followed by many *coteries* and *pays* decked out in their symbolic colors and sporting their staffs. There is also a church service for all journeymen, atheists and believers alike, who wish to honor Joseph, the carpenter of Nazareth. The journeyman carpenters of the *devoirs* are then received by the mayor of Toulouse in the majestic Salle des Illustres, or Hall of Worthies, an occasion marked by speeches of reciprocal homage. The festival, beloved of *soubises*, *indiens*, and *chiens-loups*, is brought to a fitting close by a great banquet.

> Friends of good red wine
> Let us lift our glasses three times
> Friends, let us drink to our health
> And empty all our glasses.
>
> —Nineteenth-century table song
> for Saint Joseph's Day

Journeyman *Mères*

Evidence of the vitality of journeyman culture in Toulouse is provided by a simple fact: within a few years' time, each of the city's journeyman organizations has inducted a new *mère*. On June 20 and 21, 1986, the Association Ouvrière des Compagnons du Devoir bestowed the status of *mère* on Madame Saffon. The solemn reception of a woman who has long pondered this serious commitment is always a privileged moment in the life of a journeyman community. In the case of the Association Ouvrière, candidates begin as a *dame économe*, or housekeeper, after which they attain the intermediate status of *dame-hôtesse*, or lady-hostess. During this probationary period the young woman can become familiar with the daily life of the chapter house, just as the journeyman can assess the qualities of the candidate. An article in the periodical *Compagnonnage* about the reception of *mère* Saffon by *Parisien la Volonté* (The Determined One from Paris) contains the following revealing lines, applicable to all *mères* on the Tour de France:

> If you can love without playing favorites; if you can welcome one and all, at any given moment, with warmth; if you can prepare, or have prepared, 40 to 200 meals a day, 300 days a year; if you can keep your house clean, despite the daily presence of restless young men; if you are able to sense fatigue, illness, and discouragement; if you know how to be solicitous without being overbearing; if you know how to advise and offer support with discretion; if you can put up with a house that is always bustling with new faces; if you never neglect the demanding management responsibilities entrusted to you; if you are

Right: **Madam Saffon**, *mère* of journeymen of the *devoir* in Toulouse

Below: **Group portrait taken during the 1980 Saint Joseph's Day celebration of journeyman carpenters of the *devoirs*, organized by the Toulouse chapter of the Fédération Compagnonnique des Métiers du Bâtiment**

good, just, and firm for all those around you; if you are the center of a thriving community without anyone suspecting it; if your own family is never sacrificed; if, despite vexations and disappointments, you always try to keep smiling and keep lines of communication open . . . then, you can be a journeyman *mère*.

The position of *mère*, while immensely important to every journeyman chapter on the Tour de France, is incredibly demanding, which explains the scarcity of serious candidates. Thus one can easily imagine how joyous an occasion it was for the Fédération Compagnonnique of Toulouse when, on July 1, 1990, it celebrated the reception of a new carpenters' *mère*, Madame Dejuge. Here again, the occasion was marked by great solemnity. Unlike the other journeyman organizations, the Fédération Compagnonnique perpetuates the tradition of affiliating its *mères* with a specific craft. In concrete terms, this does not make for any significant differences in the daily life of the house, for, in Toulouse as elsewhere, she performs her welcoming duties with equal solicitude for all members of the community. In Toulouse, then, the *mères* Saffon and Dejuge occupy posts that have figured in journeyman culture for several centuries: the earliest known mention of the existence of a *mère* dates from 1540.

The functions performed by *mères* are by no means subsidiary or merely ceremonial. They, too, receive symbolic colors: white, to symbolize the sacred quality of their charge.

The *Rouleur*

The other essential figure in the daily life of a journeyman house is known as the *rouleur*. This post is occupied by the journeymen on a rotating basis. Its responsibilities have changed somewhat over time. In the past, the *rouleur* greeted new arrivals, entered their names in a special book, known as the *rôle*, and saw to it that they found work in one of the city's workshops. In many respects, modern *rouleurs* resemble masters of ceremony; while they still fulfill the functions just described, these have been much altered, for the human relations so dear to journeymen in the past have been profoundly affected by the advent of the telephone and personal computers. A *rouleur* also presides over journeyman festivals and assemblies. Using the beribboned staff that distinguishes him from other journeymen, he can impose silence on the assembled company. It falls to him to make sure that all rules are obeyed. His presence at ritual and symbolic ceremonies—adoptions, receptions, "completions," chains of alliance—is indispensable. He also leads processions through the city (*rouler* means both "to rotate" and "to lead"). In some journeyman organizations, he wears a top hat as another indicator of his function. A kind of unifying link between the various hierarchical components of the journeyman community, the *rouleur* is, with the *mère*, a guarantor of the proper operation of the chapter house, although more organizations are now paying administrators to assume some of these responsibilities.

Marseille le 15 avril 1838

Je m'engage à tenir aux compagnons et
aspirant tourneurs une chambre et tout le nécessaire
de plus recevoir malle et lettre qui me seront
adressées et faire les avances du transport pour les
compagnons et aspirant si un autre corps d'état
ami adressait une malle chez moi la retireraient
la même chose et de ne recevoir aucun corps d'état
chez moi qui vous seraient nuisible ———

De plus je m'engage de faire les avances de
la nouriture a crédit vingt cinq franc pour un
compagnon et quinze francs pour un aspirant que la
société s'engage à me repondre tout compagnon qu
aspirant qui me laisseront des dette ne serait il que cinq
francs je garderait leurs effet jusqu'à la solde auquel je
remettrai les effets de suite — — — — —
si dans tous les cas je ne seraient pas content de vous je
vous avertiraient trois mois d'avance — — — —

Guis

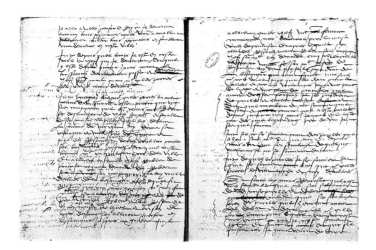

Left: **Contract of a *mère* of the journeyman turners of the *devoir* in Marseilles, 1838**

Opposite: **Journeyman assembly proceedings from Dijon, 1540, page containing the oldest known mention of a journeyman *mère*, or chapter-house mother**

Right: **In some journeyman organizations, the *rouleurs* wear top hats with wide ribbons wound around them.**

The Rule of Journeyman Carpenters of the *Devoir* on the Tour de France

If you enter the dining room in the regional headquarters of the Fédération Compagnonnique in Toulouse, you can read the Rule binding on journeyman carpenters of the *devoirs*. Like the Rules of other journeyman organizations, they tell us much about the spirit of the *devoir:*

This Rule is the fruit of experience in journeyman houses and serves the community for the good of all.

1. All young men arriving in a journeyman house must obey these rules. All aspirants or journeymen arriving at the chapter must first greet the *mère* as well as the host and the "little sister."

2. Subject to fines: anyone calling the *mère* "madame." If she has not yet been received a *mère*, she is to be addressed as *dame-hôtesse*. Anyone addressing the "little sister" as "mademoiselle" or "servant" will also be subject to fines. Likewise those who address a *coterie* or a *pays* as "monsieur."

3. Dress at the table is to be proper, with a tie, a napkin, a jacket, and clean clothing; language there must be purged of all vulgar expressions. *Patoise* and speaking with a lowered voice, and all discussion of politics and religion are forbidden, as is all animated discussion. Likewise, anyone who arrives late without a legitimate excuse, stains the table, or dirties the floor will be subject to fines.

4. All *coteries* and *pays* who damage the property of the house or the school will be subject to serious fines, and their case may be brought before an assembly for discussion. There is to be no rowdiness in the evening.

5. All *coteries* and *pays* who show a lack of respect for the *mère* or the "little sister" will be obliged to leave the house if they have not yet been received a journeyman or an aspirant. If otherwise, their case will be judged by the elders; this is a grave infraction requiring more serious disciplinary action than a fine.

6. All *coteries* and *pays* must faithfully attend classes for four years, unless freed of this obligation after assessment of their progress. All absences are subject to fines. The *rouleur* is responsible for keeping track of attendance. Paying a fine does not fully compensate for breaking a rule.

7. These rules must be freely accepted and everyone must adhere to them without resentment. A *rouleur* selected from the journeymen and aspirants will be charged with making sure that they are obeyed. All *coteries* and *pays* who, after several infractions, cannot adhere to them will be sent away from the house.

This Rule was made official by the Congress of Bordeaux in 1957, and is thus binding on all houses.

Since 1957, some of these articles have been excised or changed. It is no longer obligatory, for example, to wear a tie when eating in the dining hall of a journeyman house. *Compagnonnage* is an institution that has survived for centuries because it has been able to adapt to changing attitudes and mores. Politeness and courtesy are still required, however, just as political and religious differences must be left at the door of journeyman venues. The three journeyman families are in agreement on these requirements, which have always been central to communal life on the Tour de France.

La Jolie Ville: Bordeaux

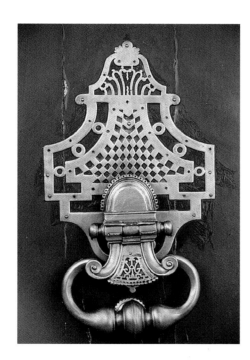

BORDEAUX

Bordeaux, *la jolie ville,*
Ah! The charming sojourn
The *Devoir* obliges us
To pay it a visit.

According to journeyman legend, Bordeaux, the *jolie ville* (pretty city) sung by the *devoirants*, welcomed Father Soubise when he returned to the West after having completed the Temple in Jerusalem. Thus the capital of the Gironde is especially dear to journeymen of this rite, the famous *bons drilles* (good fellows), children of Father Soubise (carpenters, roofers, plaster workers). Bordeaux was also long considered one of the four principal cities on the Tour de France of journeymen of the *devoir* professing the rite of Master Jacques.

Among the many famous men elevated here to the status of journeyman was Ferdinand Flouret, who in 1872 became a journeyman wheelwright under the symbolic name *Dauphiné l'Espérance* (The Hope of Dauphiné). Even today, the work of Ferdinand Flouret elicits the admiration of connoisseurs, with its mastery of formidable technical difficulties. In 1901, Abel Boyer was elevated to the rank of journeyman farrier of the *devoir* by the Bordeaux chapter, which gave him the symbolic name *Périgord Coeur Loyal* (Loyal Heart of Périgord). This *pays* would distinguish himself as a syndicalist leader of the farriers and, above all, as the moving force behind *Les Muses du tour de France*, an encyclopedia of *compagnonnage* published in 1925. Finally, we note that in 1939, the young Jean Bernard was received here as an itinerant stonecutter of the *devoir* under the name *La Fidélité d'Argenteuil* (The Faithful One from Argenteuil). He was responsible for establishing the Association Ouvrière des Compagnons du Devoir du Tour de France.

Opposite: **Rule of the Bordeaux chapter of the journeyman wheelwrights of the *devoir*, 1860**

Above: **Journeyman joiners sometimes call Bordeaux "the city of doors." Here, a splendid knocker, Hôtel de Lalande**

LES COMPAGNONS PASS: CHAR-

CADICHONNE
PLEURANT LE
DEPART D'UN
BORDELLE

Above: **The Bordeaux chapter house of the journeymen of the** *devoir*

Preceding pages: **Étienne Leclair, painting of a** *conduite*, **or ritual departure procession, of a journeyman on the Tour de France, 1826**

Right: **Certificate testifying to membership of a journeyman baker in the Bordeaux journeyman chapter, 1810**

Consolidating the Chapter Houses

When consulting the archives about the establishment of a journeyman community in a given city, it is always instructive to study attempts made to improve relations between organizations devoted to different crafts. Such research must, of course, be based on reliable documents. Here again, police records provide a useful complement to journeyman documents.

In 1901, there were fifteen different addresses of the Bordeaux chapter houses listed as serving journeymen professing the rites of Father Jacques and Father Soubise. All of these were for only one of the *devoirs*. At the same time, the *devoir de liberté* and the young Union Compagnonnique des Devoirs Unis also had a few *cayennes* and *chambres* in the city of Bordeaux and its suburbs. In fact, such a varied list is typical of the way journeyman organizations were organized in the past, which differs markedly from how they are structured today.

For centuries, journeyman houses tended to be specific to a single craft. These venues were not so much headquarters as inns where newly arrived journeymen lodged and socialized. They were operated by a woman who could attain the title of journeyman *mère*—or *père*, father, if they were male—if they contracted to perform the requisite duties with a specific local craft chapter, for there was no question of several rites sharing a single inn.

Increasingly, crafts agreed to share the same *mère*, primarily as an economic measure. In this regard, the case of Bordeaux is especially interesting. The decision made by the locksmiths and the cobblers to share quarters on rue Roquelaure was not based on any aspect of journeyman tradition. The same holds, conversely, for the *soubises* journeymen—carpenters, roofers, plaster workers—who preferred to maintain separate venues. But in some cases the craft groupings seem to make more sense. The blacksmiths, founders, tin workers, and cutlers, all of which are listed at the same address, constituted a single organization known as the *quatre corps*, or four corporations.

In Bordeaux, as elsewhere, such regroupings became more common in the early twentieth century, when the *quatre corps* were joined by the plasterers and joiners: their location became the city's principal journeyman venue. This development marks an important turning point in the history of *compagnonnage*. In the midst of an identity crisis and facing a decline in new members, the various journeyman organizations realized that reforms would be necessary in order for the institution to survive. Craft-specific chapter houses were no longer realistic. Like the journeyman Bonvous, those concerned about the future of *compagnonnage* tried to imagine another form, another project, another structure that would be better adapted to the modern world. World War II accelerated these important changes on the Tour de France.

Left: **Letter from the** *premier en ville* **of the journeyman wheelwrights of Bordeaux, 1808**

Below: **Pediment relief in the Place de la Bourse (formerly the Place Royale) alluding to the rivalry between** *loups* **and** *loups-garous* **stonecutters during construction of the project**

Henceforth, journeyman chapter houses gathered several crafts under the same roof. Since the 1950s, each of the three French journeyman organizations has organized a network of houses on their respective Tours. Each itinerant, whatever his craft, is lodged, fed, and trained in venues shared by all the crafts. Masons, carpenters, stonecutters, plumbers, roofers, and joiners now cohabit in comfortable, functional facilities that are quite different from the inns of old. In addition to dormitory rooms and kitchens, today's chapter houses usually have administrative offices, workshops, classrooms, a library, a bar, and a "masterpiece" room.

The Union Compagnonnique does not presently have a chapter house in Bordeaux, but the other two French journeyman organizations do: the Fédération Compagnonnique des Métiers du Bâtiment and the *prévôté* of the Association Ouvrière des Compagnons du Devoir du Tour de France.

The Place Royale

The current Place de la Bourse, formerly the Place Royale, was built between 1729 and 1765 by the famous architects Jacques V Gabriel and his son Anges-Jacques Gabriel. Chosen by King Louis XV, the architects had discussions with both journeyman stonecutters of the *devoir* and with those of the *étranger* rite before deciding which group would be best suited to the project. They awarded the commission to the *étrangers*.

The *étrangers* spent many months conscientiously cutting and sizing many stones. Then came the moment of laying the stone, and something extraordinary happened: the stones prepared by the *étrangers* did not align properly and the keystones of the arches could not be set. Unable to solve the problem, the *étrangers*, who were utterly humiliated, had to surrender the commission to the rival stonecutters of the *devoir*, to whom the architects now turned.

According to oral tradition, the *devoirants* were able to solve the problem within a matter of hours. The same tradition also holds that the *devoir* stonecutters had sabotaged the work of their rivals in order to reclaim the commission previously denied them. If this is true, their dishonest action amounted to a betrayal of the ideals of their *devoir*.

This episode found its way into the sculptural program of the square, in the form of a relief that, understandably, quickly attained the status of a *remarque*. One of the pediments of what was originally the Hôtel des Fermes, or local headquarters of the tax farmers, is adorned with a relief representing the goddess Minerva bestowing a golden crown on the square's

designers. At left, charming and robust putti are shown cheerfully cutting and measuring stones. They are surrogates for the journeyman stonecutters of the *devoir*, also known as children of Master Jacques. To Minerva's right, a crouching old man is shown pulling out his hair, a compass, a square, and a protractor lying on the ground before him. He represents the humiliated journeyman *étrangers*, depicted as old because the *étrangers* were thought to be the most venerable of all journeyman confraternities. He has abandoned his tools in despair, having fallen victim to the trap maliciously set for him by the *devoirants*.

This relief is a fine example of how some journeyman anecdotes cannot be found in history books but are engraved in stone, if one knows how to read them.

Étienne Leclair, Painter of Journeyman Subjects

The name Étienne Leclair is well known to journeymen, for in the first half of the nineteenth century he produced many naive paintings of the *conduite*, the ritual ceremony of departure performed whenever a journeyman on the Tour de France left one city for another. In addition to being an artist, Leclair was the official overseer of bridges and roadways for the city of Bordeaux. During the first decade of the nineteenth century, he produced many watercolor drawings, which he sold to journeymen as souvenirs of their Tour de France or, more specifically, of their sojourn in Bordeaux. This naive painter, whose works are now in demand, worked primarily for wheelwrights, farriers, harness makers, and linen weavers of the *devoir*. The Museum of Compagnonnage in Tours owns several paintings of *conduites* by Leclair.

Left and below: **From *L'Illustration*, 1845, two depictions of journey-man *conduites* by Jules Noël**

Opposite: **Étienne Leclair, depiction of a journeyman *conduite*, 1826**

The Conduite

Most of Leclair's compositions represent *la conduite en règle*, the ceremony of ritual departure performed when a journeyman on the Tour de France left one city for another after having successfully satisfied his obligations (*en règle* means "in order" or "having settled one's debts"). The ceremony was performed in much the same way by all the journeyman organizations. The *rouleur* led the procession, the departing journeyman or journeymen following directly behind him. All the other journeymen, wearing their colors and carrying their staffs, followed at a certain distance, in double file. Upon reaching the city gate, the *rouleur* intoned a traditional chant, with the assembled company joining in for the refrains. Outside of the city, the procession came to a halt: this was the moment of the *guilbrette*, or ritual gestures, and a few other rites of separation. Thereafter, the departing itinerant was obliged to continue forward without turning back, a sign of his determination to continue his Tour de France despite his regret at leaving behind his many new friends.

With the appearance of the railroad, automobiles, and then airplanes, the *conduite* fell into disuse. From time to time, however, this charming ritual is revived in the form of a short procession accompanying the first steps of a departing itinerant completing the Tour de France—not effected on foot since the first decades of the twentieth century:

The hour of my departure approaches,
I must stick to my resolve;
Already the *rouleur* is stepping off,
Showing me the way.

Flowering fields, gentle landscapes,
Charming valleys, radiant slopes,
Farewell, beautiful romance, lovely city,
Farewell Bordeaux! Farewell Bordeaux!
      —"Les Adieux à Bordeaux" by *Guépin l'Aimable*
(The Lovable One from Guêpe), nineteenth century

Below and right: **Songbooks and record published by the Association Ouvrière des Compagnons du Devoir du Tour de France**

Opposite: **Bernard Gautier, late-nineteenth-century caricature of a journeyman carpenter on Saint Joseph's Day**

Journeyman Songs

It is striking how many journeyman songs, old and new, allude to Bordeaux. Its port, its bridge, its Place Royale, and its beautiful women are praised often by journeyman poets. In the words of Abel Boyer, known as *Périgord le Coeur Loyal* (The Loyal Heart from Périgord):

> Journeymen often sing without art or symmetry, but they know their way around caesuras and hemistichs and their songs are always beautiful. They recount their lives, their efforts, their struggles, their disappointments, their joys, but also the crowning of their constant striving to perfect their crafts, their hearts, their minds.

In the past, most journeyman songs were about rivalries between enemy *devoirs*. But times have changed, as has *compagnonnage*. New songs still emerge from the three French journeyman families every year, for singing remains an integral part of the Tour de France. *Arrosages* ("soakings") and birthday banquets are privileged moments when *pays* and *coteries* sing, at the invitation of the *rouleur*, journeyman songs whose refrains are then taken up by the assembled company. At the banquet following their reception, new journeymen must sing to show their brothers in the *devoir* that they are capable, as the ritual formula goes.

The famous journeyman songwriters of the past— *Vendôme la Clef des Coeurs* (The Key of Hearts from Vendôme), *Le Bien Aimé de Saint-Georges de Reintembault* (The Well-Loved One from Saint-Georges de Reintembault), *Languedocien l'Ami des Filles* (The Friend of Girls from Languedoc), *Rochelais l'Enfant Chéri* (The Cherished Child of Rochelais), *Dauphiné la Clef des Coeurs* (The Key of Hearts from Dauphiné)—have been succeeded by the likes of *Périgord Coeur Loyal* (The Loyal Heart from Périgord), *La Gaieté de Villebois* (The Gaiety of Villebois), *Pierre le Saintonge* (Pierre from Saintonge), *Berry la Gaieté du Tour de France* (The Gaiety of the Tour de France from Berry), *La Fraternité de Marseille* (The Fraternity of Marseilles), *Normand la Sérénité de Gacé* (The Serenity of Gacé from Normandy), *Genevois la Fraternité de Plainpalais* (The Fraternity of Plainpalais from Geneva). Despite their differences, all are links in a long chain of *chansonniers* who have sung, are singing, and will continue to sing the glory of *compagnonnage*:

> From Saintonge in Gascogne
> Toward the sea on silver waves
> Bordeaux, the fertile mother
> Of the Midi, sets the tone.
> Its port and stone bridge
> So dear to our *devoirants*
> Sweet, short-lived memories
> We leave you singing.
> —"Sur les routes du tour de France," by
> Pierre Morin, known as *Pierre le Saintonge*
> (Pierre from Saintonge), 1932

Baptiste Gilez dit tourangeau Cœur zèle
Compagnons Sabotier du devoir reçu à
Nantes Le 15 aôu L'an 1848.

A City of the *Devoir:* Nantes

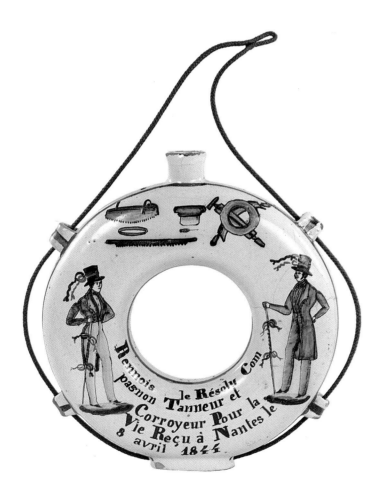

Opposite: **Painting by Paulin, painter-glazier-gilder, 1848, Edeline collection. Image commemorating the reception of** *Tourangeau Coeur Zélé* **(Zealous Heart from Touraine) as a journeyman** *sabot* **maker of the** *devoir* **in Nantes**

Above: **Canteen commemorating the reception of** *Rennois le Résolu* **(The Resolute One from Rennes), journeyman tanner of the** *devoir,* **in Nantes in 1844, Edeline collection**

NANTES

Nantes is a beautiful city, remarkable for its port, its bridges, its promenades, several monuments, among them the cathedral, other churches, the prefecture, the exchange, the theater, decorated with eight Corinthian columns. . . . On the portal of one of the churches there's a small bas-relief picturing, it is said, Mark Anthony, and in a posture that modesty prevents me from describing.

—Agricol Perdiguier, description of Nantes
in *Mémoires d'un compagnon*

As these lines suggest, Perdiguier found Nantes to be a city much like any other, save for the presence of a slightly scandalous journeyman *remarque,* the only note that sets the account apart from many others he penned from his first Tour de France.

Journeyman culture has figured in the history of the great city of the Loire country for centuries. Archival documents dating from the early nineteenth century describe it as one of the four principal cities on the Tour de France of journeymen of the *devoir,* children of Master Jacques, the other three being Paris, Lyon, and Bordeaux. This is already a telling indicator of the richness of the city's journeyman traditions.

The Hospitality of the Carmelite Monastery

In 1758, the Parlement of Brittany was indignant that journeyman joiners of the *devoir* in Nantes had succeeded in establishing a chapter in the city's Carmelite monastery, where they were holding meetings and inducting new members outside the reach of the law. Expanding upon the extant prohibition of journeyman assemblies, the parlement solemnly forbade the Carmelite monks to rent any of their facilities to journeyman organizations. This anecdote is of some historical significance, for it indicates that, a century

Opposite: **Image commemorating the reception of *Richard Cour d'Amour* as a journeyman nail-maker of the *devoir*, June 17, 1822, Edeline collection**

Above: **The current Nantes chapter house of the journeymen of the** *devoir*

Right: **The completion of a "masterpiece" is a brief, privileged moment in the life of a journeyman. His real "masterpiece" will consist in his continuing to produce work infused with a love of his craft.**

after the famous condemnation of *compagnonnage* by the theology faculty of the Sorbonne in Paris, the monks in Nantes were prepared to ignore the excommunication levied against journeymen on the Tour de France. With all deliberation, it seems the Carmelite monastery had decided to help out a journeyman organization, one whose membership was exclusively Catholic.

The example of the Carmelite monastery makes it easier for us to understand the material organization of the many groups affiliated with the *devoir*—or, to use the phrase that makes their Catholic character explicit, with the *Saint-Devoir de Dieu* (Sacred Duty to God). In the turbulent eighteenth century, journeymen found ecclesiastical authorities in many cities more than willing to establish or renew the church's ties to an organization whose power was increasing, for, despite the royal prohibitions and condemnations issued repeatedly in the past, *compagnonnage* continued to thrive. Skillfully exploiting the Revocation of the Edict of Nantes (1685), the Catholic faith strove to spread its protective wing and exert its moral tutelage over a *compagnonnage* that had become deeply divided over the religious question. Thus did material assistance prove a spearhead to moral and spiritual guidance: to facilitate its control over Catholic workers looking to benefit from the privileges of *compagnonnage* (lodging, employment, solidarity, travel), the church had the idea of opening the doors of many of its monasteries to journeyman organizations that did not reject the teachings of Rome. This made it possible for the church to influence journeyman

reception ceremonies, transforming what it saw as "pagan" rituals into religious rites.

Its attempt to wipe out journeyman organizations having failed, the church altered its approach: instead of condemning the institution, it resolved to tolerate it and then shape its values and practices so as to make them more consistent with Catholic aspirations, summed up in the phrase *Saint-Devoir de Dieu*. Some regard this as sufficient to justify the existence of Father Soubise, Benedictine monk and symbol of the Christianization of *compagnonnage*. But the interpretation of myths and legends is more complex than this.

The anecdote of the Carmelite monastery can be understood in various ways. On the one hand, *compagnonnage* was at the mercy of a church skilled at subtle manipulation; on the other hand, *compagnonnage* had agreed, without giving up any of its specific qualities, to work with one of its fiercest adversaries. Such an approach to the problem, however, seems reductive. The history of relations between the French church and *compagnonnage* is complicated; examination of a far larger corpus of documents in Nantes alone would be required to do it justice. But one thing is certain: beginning in the eighteenth century, religion becomes a privileged factor in the history of journeyman organizations and relations among themselves as well as with the world around them, which they were already characterizing as "profane."

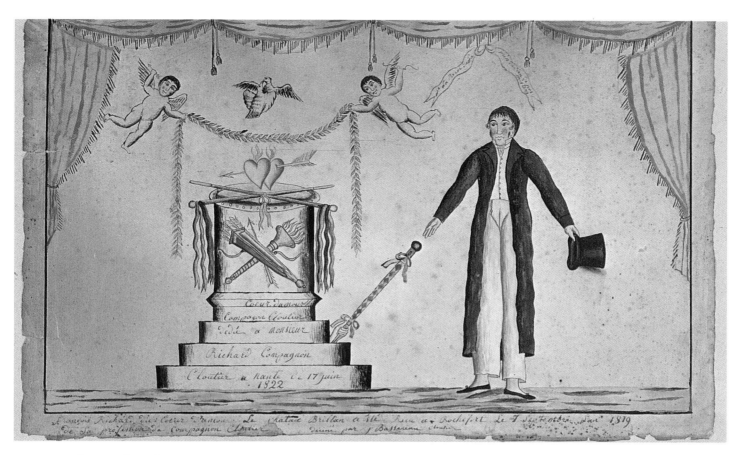

Jacques le Jambard

Journeymen joiners of the *devoir* were not the only ones to have a chapter in Nantes. In this same period, the journeyman joiners *non du devoir* (later of the *devoir de liberté)* also had a chapter there, as evidenced by their precious *rolle* of 1765, now on exhibit in the Museum of Compagnonnage in Tours.

The *rolle* was a ritual volume in which were inscribed, among other things, an organization's rules and the names of newly arrived itinerants. The *rolle* kept by the *gavots* of Nantes is bound in leather with colored stamps that include a square and compass, a portrait of Louis XV, and a caricature of Master Jacques (the protector of journeyman joiners of the *devoir*) with the following caption: "Effigy of *Jacque[s] le Jambar[d]* famous *devoirant* executed from life the evening he was burned in a clear fire for having offended against the king [*pronostiqué contre un Royalle*]." These lines confirm that, already in the middle of the eighteenth century, Master Jacques was identified as Jacques de Molay, the last grand master of the Knights Templar, who was burned alive on the orders of Philip the Fair.

Some Celebrities

The city of Nantes is associated with the memory of several journeymen who left their mark on the history of the *devoirs* in various ways. A case in point is Auguste Batard, whose Tour de France extended from 1887 to 1891; he was received a journeyman harness maker of the *devoir* under the symbolic name *Nantais la Belle Conduite* (The Beautiful *Conduite* of Nantes). This great figure of *compagnonnage* in Nantes wrote a short

memoir entitled *À l'école du courage et du savoir* (At the school of the courage and knowledge) in which he managed to convey the essence of the journeyman calling. His text bears the following dedication:

> To my children, in whom I wanted to instill
> a taste for work well done.
> To my grandchildren, that they might continue the tradition.
> To my great grandchildren, so that they might receive it
> and transmit it in their turn.

In 1880, Jules Delhomme, journeyman rope maker of the *devoir*, known as *Coeur Content le Bordelais* (The Contented Heart from Bordeaux), established a pension and assistance fund that, after being consolidated with that of the journeymen of Tours, became well known under the name *Ralliement des compagnons du devoir et chevaliers de l'ordre de maître Jacques et du père Soubise* (Rallying point of Journeymen of the *Devoir* and Knights of the Order of Master Jacques and Father Soubise). Delhomme's work continues to bear fruit today, for the Ralliement still exists and has aided many journeymen. Its headquarters are in the Nantes chapter house of the Association Ouvrière des Compagnons du Devoir du Tour de France. In this context, it is worth noting that *compagnonnage* played an important role in the establishment of such institutions for cooperative financial support in French life. In 1991, the Mutualité Française sponsored the publication of a book by Jean-Pierre Duroy entitled *Le Compagnonnage aux sources*

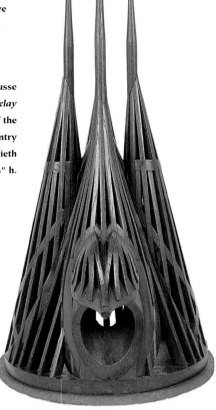

Left: **Classes given at journeyman chapter houses aim to improve the students' mastery of their craft at a pace that best suits their abilities.**

Right: **Michel Ramousse (1881–1946), known as *Velay l'Ami du Trait* (The Friend of the *Trait* from Velay), carpentry "masterpiece," early twentieth century, walnut, 21⅜" h.**

de l'économie sociale (*Compagnonnage* and the origins of social economy), another indication of the link between economy and *compagnonnage*.

Another celebrity received in Nantes was Emmanuel Colomp (1821–1893), who became a journeyman rope maker of the *devoir* under the symbolic name *L'Estimable le Provençal* (The Estimable One from Provence). This songwriter, well known in his own day, remains a presence on the Tour de France for two of his songs, *La Mort du Provençal* (The Death of the Man from Provence) and *La Provençale* (The Man from Provence), are often sung at journeyman banquets:

Let my colors be brought to me this instant,
I want to see them before rendering my soul,
Dear journeymen, lay them over my heart,
That they might serve as my *oriflamme.*
I will retain them as far as the tomb
To prove my love and my devotion,
And when my heart gives out,
Try, my son, to be, through your knowledge,
A journeyman on the Tour de France.

—*La Mort du Provençal*

Another remarkable man was received in Nantes on Saint Joseph's Day in 1837. The city's chapter of the journeyman carpenters of the *devoir* of Father Soubise received the *coterie* Jean Danis under the symbolic name *Moissac la Belle Conduite* (The Beautiful *Conduite* from Moissac). In fact, he rapidly became

known as *Moissac la Pipe* (The Pipe from Moissac), having become famous on the Tour de France for his plush two-cornered hat and especially for a curious pipe with secret compartments that he had made. It was devised such that he could take snuff, chew tobacco, and even drink while smoking.

The Three Levels of *Compagnonnage*

Before aspiring to the title of journeyman, young craftsmen intending to complete a Tour de France must first decide on their organizational affiliation. In the past, this choice was determined by family tradition. Furthermore, religious considerations were of primary concern until the early twentieth century. Finally, the geographic accessibility of a journeyman organization had to be taken into account. Today things are very different. Religious factors no longer influence a decision that, increasingly, is more a matter of chance than the result of serious reflection. The decision might be affected by an advertisement, an article in the press, or a poster, and it might even be taken unconsciously without the youngster's being familiar with other journeyman organizations. Then again, in the case of some crafts there are no other options. Cooks, for example, are acknowledged only by the Union Compagnonnique des Devoirs Unis. Aspiring bakers cannot turn to the Fédération Compagnonnique des Métiers du Bâtiment, for this organization is limited to the building trades. On the other hand, young carpenters wishing to become journeymen are faced with an embarrassment of riches, for their craft is recognized by all three organizations. In other words, all of the building

Jules Noël, "The Reception," print from *L'Illustration*, 1845, depicting a reception ceremony. Traditionally, one must submit a "masterpiece" to critical scrutiny in order to qualify for the title "journeyman of the Tour de France." If the candidate's "masterpiece" is deemed acceptable, he is authorized for reception. Today's reception ceremonies differ from those in the nineteenth century, but they are performed in the same spirit, leaving a solemn and indelible mark on the memory of newly received journeymen.

trades are welcome in all of the journeyman families, but for other crafts it is very unlikely that one will be able to choose from three possible organizational affiliations.

After selecting an organization, one must set about qualifying for the first status on the route to becoming a journeyman. This entails spending several months at one or more journeyman houses preparing a small work known as a maquette or *travail d'adoption*. When this maquette is deemed acceptable, its maker is accorded the status of aspirant or affiliate, and awarded the corresponding colors. Thereafter, he can pursue his Tour de France by working in various cities where his organization is represented. Currently, the Tour can last from three to seven years, depending on the organization. As a general rule, time must be spent in a minimum of five cities before one can present a "masterpiece" in hopes of being received.

The fashioning of a "masterpiece" is at the core of the Tour de France. Itinerant journeymen acquire bits and pieces of experience in town after town, the ultimate result being a rich harvest of knowledge. The journeyman's "masterpiece" is the fruit of this experience and of many hundreds of hours' work performed in his free time. The long-awaited day of presentation coincides, whenever possible, with the name day of the patron of the young man's craft. Thus journeymen carpenters are usually received on March 19, Saint Joseph's Day, journeymen joiners on Saint Anne's Day, etc. The reception ceremony begins with a critique, in the course of which a group of journeymen selected by the president of the *cayenne* or *cham-*

bre (terms for a local chapter, depending on the craft) assesses the work and puts forth questions to the candidate. If the jury and the assembled company are satisfied with the quality of the work and the worker, the ritual can proceed, at the end of which the aspirant is officially acknowledged a journeyman on the Tour de France. We leave it to *Nantais le Soutien des Bons Drilles* (The Stay of the "Good Fellows" from Nantes) not to reveal but to suggest the content of this ceremony, which is a significant event for the newly received journeyman:

> When the evening arrived I underwent the trial
> Compass in hand I demonstrated my talents
> Having given proof of my knowledge
> Having promised to keep my oaths
> I was admitted into the great family.
> In memory of my reception
> I was named "The Stay of the *Bons Drilles*"
> Could any journeyman name be more beautiful?
> —"L'Heureux Bon Drille," journeyman song from 1912

Many journeyman songs, especially those from the nineteenth century, allude to the reception ceremony without providing details about it. Whether old or new, all of them evoke the two pillars of the ceremony: the trials and the oath. After the ceremony has ended, the journeyman can brandish his colors and his staff, signs of his status and his title:

Above: **A modern *carré* of the Association Ouvrière des Compagnons du Devoir du Tour de France**

Left: **From the moment they enter the journeyman world, young men are asked to familiarize themselves with the Rule of their organization. Here, journeymen of the *devoir* listen as a candidate reads a portion of it aloud.**

But one fine evening, with a fearful heart,
I presented myself to the journeymen
I swore to Master Jacques that I would
Fulfill my obligations, always and unstintingly
Thus I, too, had the sweet happiness
Of proudly wearing our beautiful colors
Now and forever
I dedicate my love to them.
—"Nos Belles Couleurs," song by P. Aubard,
known as *Berry la Gaieté du Tour de France*
(The Gaeity of the Tour de France from Berry)

Not all received journeymen attain the third level of *compagnonnage:* a "finished" journeyman. Some organizations bestow this status only after the successful presentation of another "masterpiece," one whose quality indicates that the journeyman has progressed still further in the knowledge and mastery of his craft. Other organizations waive this requirement, holding that this symbolic elevation is an acknowledgment of the man's human qualities, an indication that his comportment and actions are likely to foster the spread of *compagnonnage.* After adoption and reception comes completion, the third symbolic ceremony marking the progress along the path of *compagnonnage.*

The Association Ouvrière des Compagnons du Devoir du Tour de France defines the three levels of journeyman life as follows:

1. aspirant (*aspirant*): a young man whose consciousness is being prepared

2. received journeyman (*compagnon reçu*): a man whose consciousness is open to his craft

3. finished journeyman (*compagnon fini*): a man whose consciousness is open to his fellow men

The *Carré*

From the moment of a candidate's "adoption" until his eventual "completion," every step he takes along the path of his profession is recorded on a document that most organizations now call the *carré,* or square. In the past, this journeyman "passport" has been known by various names: *affaire* (business), *cheval* (horse), *navire* (vessel), *arriat* (folded sail), *mouton* (sheep). Until the last century, *carrés* were rich in symbolism and bore many coded initials; today they are much simpler, having been shorn of the excessive symbolism typical of the second half of the nineteenth century.

Today, the *carré* always accompanies an itinerant during his Tour de France, being entrusted to the local journeymen as soon as he arrives in a chapter. This sheet, which when folded is shaped like a square, generally bears the signatures of those in authority at the chapter where the young man was "adopted" as well as the stamps of the chapters where he has sojourned during his Tour. Occasionally, remarks about the itinerant's comportment are also recorded on it. It is surrendered to the journeyman himself only after he has completed

Like *compagnonnage* as a whole, leatherworkers and metalworkers have managed to reconcile tradition with modernity. Such adaptive facility is one of the great strengths of the journeyman movement, which, far from being an anachronism, looks toward the future.

his Tour de France. Upon the holder's death, the *carré* is rarely kept by his family. Tradition dictates that it be burned, or perhaps deposited in the archives of the deceased journeyman's chapter.

The Manor House of La Haultière

All three French journeyman organizations are represented in the city of Nantes, an indication of the city's strong journeyman traditions. Members of the *devoir* affiliated with the Association Ouvrière gather on the quai Malakoff, while the Fédération Compagnonnique des Métiers du Bâtiment has its regional headquarters on rue de l'Indre. The Union Compagnonnique des Devoirs Unis, present in Nantes since 1890, has managed after many years to restore a venue that must now be numbered among the finest facilities of this journeyman family: the manor house of La Haultière.

Owned by the Union Compagnonnique since 1968, La Haultière is situated in an old suburb of Nantes. Dating from the fourteenth century, the building has been recently restored by *pays* of the organization, who generously donated the thousands of man-hours required. In addition to serving the usual needs of a *cayenne* (ceremonies of adoption, reception, and completion, journeyman celebrations), it also houses a public museum of "masterpieces" and old tools. One of the assembly rooms, named after Agricol Perdiguier, contains a fascinating collection of journeyman documents and artifacts.

We could not conclude this discussion of the Nantes chapter of the Union Compagnonnique without mentioning an exhibition it organized in 1988, under the beguiling title "The Saga of Sugar" (*La saga du sucre*). In the course of the exhibition, the journeymen of the Union executed a gigantic model made entirely of sugar cubes—no less than 38,000—of the port of Nantes as it appeared in the eighteenth century. Not surprisingly, this extraordinary "masterpiece" was deemed worthy of inclusion in *The Guinness Book of World Records*.

The Memory of *Compagnonnage:* Tours

Above: **The Museum of Compagnonnage in Tours receives an increasing number of visitors each year.**

Opposite: **Sign for the Museum of Compagnonnage by Pierre Reynal, journeyman locksmith of the Devoirs Unis**

TOURS

Of Touraine the ancient capital,
Tours, witness to my success,
I still remember your rue Royale
The very picture of beauty, art, and progress
Cherished city of our Tour de France,
I think of you night and day,
I've always hoped to see you again
Farewell Touraine, farewell wondrous abode.

—L. P. Journolleau, known as
Rochelais l'Enfant Chéri
(The Beloved Child of Rochelle),
verse from a song, 1870

This verse includes a descriptive phrase that remains current, for Tours is still known as the *ville chérie*, or cherished city, of the Tour de France. The capital of Touraine is a journeyman city of such rare qualities that journeymen sometimes refer to it as "the Mecca of *compagnonnage*," a characterization often encountered in journeyman writings. As with Paris, Lyon, Bordeaux, and Toulouse, an entire book would be required to do justice to the city's rich journeyman heritage.

At present, the departmental seat of Indre-et-Loire is known for its Museum of Compagnonnage, now an essential stop on the Tour de France and a major attraction for anyone with an interest in journeyman culture. But even before the establishment of this remarkable museum, Touraine boasted a prestigious journeyman past in which Tours plays the leading role.

Compagnonnage has always thrived in the Loire Valley. Like all large French cities traversed by a great river, Tours has never lost touch with its journeyman traditions, maintaining its status as a city of the *devoir*. Inhabitants of Touraine still have reason to be proud, for the city has chapters of all three

journeyman organizations. Whether fulfilling the obligations of their Tour de France or simply interested in *compagnonnage*, visitors will find themselves welcome at either of the two houses of the Association Ouvrière, and at the local venues for the Fédération Compagnonnique and the Union Compagnonnique des Devoirs Unis.

In the Age of the Alliance

Founded September 6, 1908, the Alliance Compagnonnique de Tours, also known as the Fédération d'Indre-et-Loire, managed to bring together some three hundred journeymen professing the rites of Soubise and Jacques. Given that *compagnonnage* was then in the midst of its most serious identity crisis, such a project was of considerable importance. Quite influential between the two World Wars, the Alliance helped to administer the Société Protectrice des Apprentis (SPA), an organization then establishing chapters in many French cities in hopes of drawing greater attention to artisanal traditions and institutions.

In most of the SPA chapters, including Tours, a hundred apprentices were offered classes in carpentry, roofing, joinery, tinkering, plastering, locksmithing, stonecutting, and wheelwrighting. The classes were taught by journeymen of all rites—Solomon, Jacques, and Soubise—who, setting aside their differences, seized this remarkable opportunity to influence young men who might undertake a Tour de France. In Tours, as in other cities with SPA chapters, *compagnonnage* was

officially recognized by the public authorities, gaining access to a veritable hothouse for the cultivation of the institution's future.

The Alliance Compagnonnique de Tours was extremely dynamic, collaborating with business and craft groups as well as organizing many exhibitions in the Touraine region. In 1932, thanks to the gift of a cooper, the Alliance became the owner of a building on the Place des Halles, another historic site in the history of *compagnonnage* in Tours. The organization's expenses were covered by gifts, fees, and subventions. It would be impossible to overestimate the importance of the Alliance in sustaining *compagnonnage* at a time when it was on the verge of disappearing. After World War II, the Tours Alliance ceased its independent activities and, like most other such organizations, merged with the Association Ouvrière des Compagnons du Devoir.

Opposite, left: **"Masterpiece" of farriership completed in 1965 by François Bernadet, known as *Toulousain le Bien Aimé* (The Well-Loved One from Toulouse), journeyman farrier of the *devoir*, at the age of seventy-six. A miniature temple to its maker's craft, it is composed of 1,062 pieces, assembled over some 1,800 hours.**

Opposite, right: **Nineteenth-century statuette of a journeyman. Such figures, molded from plaster and then painted, survive in large numbers. They were originally placed on counters and shelves in chapter houses.**

Left: **Watercolor drawing by Besnard, known as *Angevin la Fidélité* (The Faithful One from Anjou), journeyman roofer of the *devoir*, 1848**

The *Ralliement*

In October of 1883 the first issue was published in Tours of a periodical that was to become famous throughout France, the *Ralliement des compagnons du devoir et chevaliers de l'Ordre, organe de la caisse de retraite et des intérêts compagnonniques de devoir.* Its editor was a journeyman weaver, Pierre Vauchez, known as *Comtois l'Ami des Arts* (The Friend of the Arts from Comté), whose goal was to establish a true pension fund for all members of the journeyman organizations affiliated with the *devoir*. He hoped that it would become a means of reconciling journeymen opposed to the philosophy of the young Union Compagnonnique, then in the process of being formed. Although there was competition that emerged momentarily between Tours and Nantes, where another journeyman of the *devoir*, Jules Delhomme, was trying to launch a similar enterprise, the mutual aid society soon became unified and managed to field the many problems that it had to face during its first years.

Officially registered at the prefecture of Loire-Inférieure on November 11, 1880, the *Ralliement des compagnons du devoir et chevaliers de l'Ordre de maître Jacques et du père Soubise* still exists. As in the past, the two cities that originated the project collaborate in running the organization. Their momentary competition explains the distribution of the organization's operating facilities: the administrative offices are in Tours while the client offices are in Nantes. It is hopeful that this worthy enterprise will continue to thrive.

Portraits of Journeymen

In addition to Vauchez, Touraine guards the memory of several *pays* and *coteries* who left their mark on the history of *compagnonnage*, such as Joseph Voisin, journeyman carpenter of the *devoir de liberté*, a native of Cognac who settled in Touraine after completing his Tour de France. Between 1908 and 1911, he helped to administer the Alliance Compagnonnique. A gifted carpenter and a strong personality, *Angoumois l'Ami du Trait* (The Friend of the *Trait* from Angoulême) was also the honorary president of the superior council of the *devoir de liberté*, the entity that directs the *indiens* at the national level. Opposed to the reconciliation of the rites that seemed to be emerging, in 1931 he published *Histoire de ma vie ou 55 ans de compagnonnage* (The story of my life, or fifty-five years of *compagnonnage*), a book that occasioned much controversy. Involuntarily, Joseph Voisin had just ruined a project crucial to the future of *compagnonnage*. After the book's appearance, rancor between the various journeyman organizations reasserted itself, rendering moot all attempts to reconcile them.

Another personality of the *pays* was Pierre Petit (1910–1985). Named the finest worker in France in 1972, he was received, thanks to a special dispensation, a journeyman glazier of the Devoirs Unis under the symbolic name *Tourangeau le Disciple de la Lumière* (The Disciple of Light from Touraine). He was then sixty-four years old. He is responsible for the superb stained-glass windows in the grotto in Sainte-Baume, as well as for those representing the three

legendary founders in the Museum of Compagnonnage in Tours. This master glazier, respected and admired by journeymen of all rites, painted the motto of Perdiguier on the wall of his workshop: "May all noble hearts unite, the reign of love is at hand." He died on August 29, 1985, after an automobile accident.

Unfortunately, this discussion of journeymen from Touraine must be cut short, for it would be impossible to do justice to the subject in the space available here. But *devoirants* (Vauchez), *indiens* (Voisin), and the Union Compagnonnique (Petit) as well as the various French journeyman sensibilities are embodied by these three men. In any case, it should be pointed out that, at their congress in Tours in 1930, the journeyman carpenters of Father Soubise decided to prohibit the use of the three points so as not to be confused with the *indiens* and the Freemasons. We should also mention that Tours was the site of the first reception of two journeyman weavers, *Breton l'Example de la Sagesse* (The Example of Wisdom from Brittany) and *Agenais l'Île d'Amour* (The Island of Love from Agen), into the Devoir du Tour de France, on May 1, 1964.

The Museum of Compagnonnage

Inaugurated on March 31, 1968, and the result of an agreement between the municipality of Tours and the three French journeyman organizations, the Museum of Compagnonnage in Tours functions both as a showcase and a historical depository, a storehouse of communal memory. It is also a monument to the devotion of a great friend to journeymen, Roger Lecotté.

Born in 1889, Roger Lecotté published several books about *compagnonnage* that are considered authoritative (see the bibliography). He was also largely responsible for organizing two important exhibitions devoted to the subject: *"Paris et les compagnons du tour de France"* (Paris and the Journeymen of the Tour de France, 1951–52) and *"Le Compagnonnage vivant"* (Compagnonnage Today, 1973). Roger Lecotté died in December of 1991.

The origins of the museum date back to 1967, when, at the instigation of Jean Royer, mayor of Tours, a committee composed of representatives of all three French journeyman organizations as well as delegates representing the city of Tours asked Roger Lecotté to create a museum of *compagnonnage* in a former monks' dormitory in the convent of Saint-Julien. In addition to introducing the public to the legends and history of the *devoirs*, it was to feature displays about all manner of journeyman artifacts, traditions, and emblems, including staffs, colors, tools, "masterpieces," and imagery. From the first years of its existence, this unique museum proved a great suc-

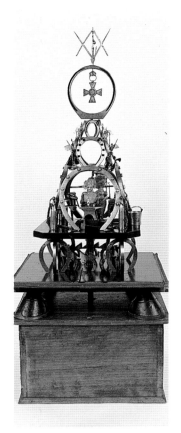

Opposite: **Detail of a stained-glass window signed by Pierre Petit, known as *Tourangeau le Disciple de la Lumière* (The Disciple of Light from Touraine). For the museum in Tours, he made three windows representing the founders of *compagnonnage*.**

Left: **Roger Lecotté giving France's president François Mitterrand a tour of the museum, February 23, 1988**

Right: **"Masterpiece" with automata by Perrot, journeyman farrier of the *devoir*, 1889**

cess. In 1973, the city of Tours built a new facility around the Romanesque wall of the former monks' hospice, and every year, tens of thousands of visitors come to admire what some have called the temple of *compagnonnage*. Journeymen, groups of students, and tourists from all over the world come in increasing numbers to the museum. It is difficult to single out specific "masterpieces" and other notable items, for the collection is rich and various. Whether journeymen or not, visitors are likely to feel that one perusal of these beautiful and informative displays is insufficient.

"This museum is not a container of dead things, a cemetery; to the contrary, it remains astonishingly vital and relevant," wrote Roger Lecotté in his visitor's guide. And it is true, there is always something new in the Museum of Compagnonnage. Every year "masterpieces" arrive to replace old ones, which are returned to their places of origin, a practice that greatly benefits returning visitors. As a result, every visit is a new voyage into the journeyman realm.

The "Masterpiece"

Historically, the first journeyman organizations were opposed to the all-powerful guilds of the Old Regime. The latter, despite the egalitarian ideals of their early years, had become a roadblock for the majority, who were effectively excluded from membership. Why, then, did the *devoirs* adopt the institution of the qualifying "masterpiece," which the guilds had used so effectively as a tool of exclusion? The answer is that all journeyman organizations deemed it essential to maintain high technical and moral standards, and the "masterpiece" trial provided an effective means of doing so.

"Masterpieces" submitted by candidates are always examined by the assembled journeymen of a charter. Detail by detail, the work is studied to assess its maker's technical proficiency, the result of his cumulative experience on the Tour de France. Questions are also put to the candidate, and his answers are taken into account in the final deliberation. If his work and comportment are found wanting, his reception is postponed until he can present a "masterpiece" worthy of the name.

Each journeyman family has its own notion of what a "masterpiece" should be. For some, "it must demonstrate a unity of conception and execution, be made entirely by hand, and be a completed object." For others, "it evidences that, for centuries, beauty has resulted not from certain well-defined canons but has emerged wherever the hand has transformed material under the guidance of an enlightened spirit." In fact,

the "masterpiece" should not be seen merely as a means of safeguarding the level of professional competence, and it is certainly never an end in itself. The process of fashioning a "masterpiece" is a trial that encourages its author to discover himself, even to blossom, by rising to the occasion presented by this exceptional challenge. During the many hours of work, the artisan often comes to understand the essential message long at the heart of journeyman culture, namely that the true "masterpiece" is not the completed object but the worker who has conceived it, designed it, and realized it. In modern-day language, we are often casual in our use of the term "masterpiece." But a visit to the museums in Tours, Troyes, and Romanèche-Thorins or to the various chapter houses on the Tour de France would suffice to remind us of the word's true meaning. A "masterpiece" is a major work marking an important step in the development of a worker trying to grow through his journeyman experiences. But it is also worth correcting a widespread misapprehension: the "masterpiece" represents only a short, privileged moment in the life of a journeyman. It is easy to understand that many journeymen are made uneasy by the prominence accorded "masterpieces" in exhibitions intended to educate the public, for it is incorrect to reduce *compagnonnage* to these artifacts, however remarkable and beautiful they might be.

There are several categories of the journeyman "masterpiece." Those produced in order to be received as a journeyman are called *chefs-d'oeuvre de réception*, or reception masterpieces. Often, before attaining the status of finished journeyman, the craftsman must present a work known as a *chef-d'oeuvre de finition*, or completion masterpiece. We have also seen that, in the past, *chefs-d'oeuvre de compétition*, or competition masterpieces, were sometimes used as a means of adjudicating competing claims to craft monopolies in a given city, specifically, in Lyon, Marseilles, and Montpellier. The lawyer Berryer, who defended the journeyman carpenters of Paris in 1845, was offered a *chef-d'oeuvre de reconnaissance* or gratitude masterpiece. At about the same time, *François le Champagne* (François from Champagne) produced a famous *chef-d'oeuvre de prestige*, or prestige masterpiece, to augment the glory and honor of journeyman joiners of the *devoir*. The journeyman farriers placed a "Saint-Eloi's bouquet" outside their workshops, otherwise known as a *chef-d'oeuvre enseigne*, or sign masterpiece, intended to demonstrate the range of their skills to potential clients. *Soubises* and *indiens* journeyman carpenters vied with one another in terms of talent and genius by making *grands chefs-d'oeuvre*, or great masterpieces, imposing productions displayed and awarded medals at countless exhibitions and national competitions.

Many retired journeymen still feel compelled to produce "masterpieces." It is moving to see these older craftsmen realize their most beautiful works in the twilight of their lives, artifacts summing up their accumulated wisdom and knowledge known in the journeyman world as *testaments à trois dimensions*, or three-dimensional testaments.

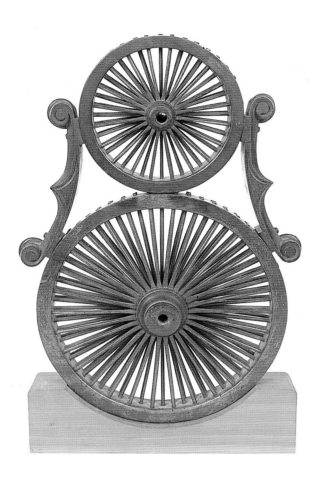

Opposite: **One of the many paint-ings of *conduites* in the Museum of Compagnonnage. This work dates from 1846.**

Left: **"Masterpiece" by a journey-man wheelwright of the *devoir***

As many Tour-de-France journeymen like to emphasize, the true "masterpiece" is not the presented work but its author, who, through the wonderfully formative and enriching trials undergone while mastering his craft, cannot but perfect himself in the process. This is one of the key lessons of *compagnonnage*.

165

THE CRAFTS

ompagnonnage derives much of its character from the fact that it encompasses only a limited number of the so-called manual crafts. Originally, it was based on the skills used by the cathedral builders. Increasingly, the institution accepted other crafts, all the while meticulously excluding those considered too alien to the art of building. Some crafts had to wait a long time before a sponsor offered to facilitate their entry into one of the journeyman families. Apart from the Union Compagnonnique, the French journeyman organizations of today still accept only a limited number of crafts.

SANCTA TRINITAS UNUS DEUS Miserere Nobis

he short texts that follow do not discuss all of the journeyman crafts, past and present. Through a more selective approach, the reader will be introduced to those crafts that have been most important in the long history of *compagnonnage*.

The earliest journeyman confraternities welcomed only artisans working with wood, stone, and iron. Gradually, crafts more remote from the tradition of the cathedral builders were accepted. Historians trying to establish the chronology of the expanding family of journeyman organizations are often hindered by lack of documentation. Journeyman archives do include hierarchical lists for each journeyman rite purporting to indicate the year of each craft's acceptance. These documents must be used with great care, however, for the dates they propose are based exclusively on oral tradition, which makes their reliability dubious. Even so, they provide us with precise lists of the accepted crafts, and they also cast welcome light on protocols that were extremely important in journeyman culture until the first decades of the twentieth century. The most widely accepted order used, for example, in ceremonial processions is as follows:

JOURNEYMEN OF THE *DEVOIR*, CHILDREN OF MASTER JACQUES

558 B.C.	Stonecutters
A.D. 570	Joiners
570	Locksmiths
1330	Dyers
1407	Rope makers
1409	Basket makers
1410	Hatters
1500	Leather dressers
1601	Founders
1603	Pin makers
1609	Ironsmiths
1700	Cloth shearers
1700	Woodturners
1701	Glaziers
1702	Saddlers
1702	Stove makers
1702	Planers
1703	Cutlers
1703	Tinsmiths
1706	Harness makers
1706	Wheelwrights
1758	Nail makers
1785	Linen weavers
1789	Farriers
1807	Shoemakers and Bootmakers
1811	Bakers
1834	Weavers
1865	*Sabot* makers

JOURNEYMEN OF THE *DEVOIR* CHILDREN OF FATHER SOUBISE

A.D. 560	Carpenters
1703	Roofers
1797	Plaster workers

JOURNEYMEN OF THE *DEVOIR DE LIBERTÉ* CHILDREN OF SOLOMON

558 B.C.	Stonecutters
A.D. 560	Carpenters
570	Joiners
570	Locksmiths
1811	Bakers
1830	Coopers
1845	Shoemakers and Bootmakers

It bears repeating that the earliest dates indicated here are without historical foundation. Beginning in the eighteenth century, however, the dates are reasonably accurate. Since the second half of the nineteenth century, when these lists were created, the landscape of *compagnonnage* has been considerably transformed. Many crafts did not survive the Industrial Revolution, with the introduction of mechanization and other technological advances. The more archaic crafts have gradually disappeared, unable to adapt or transform themselves. Modern *compagnonnage* welcomes such workers as mechanics, makers of automobile bodies, upholsterers, lead and zinc workers, and electricians. While some organizations remain faithful to tradition, admitting only practitioners of the building trades and craftsmen with venerable guild histories, the Union Compagnonnique has been quite innovative, choosing to accept professions far removed from the traditional journeyman lists, for example jewelers, chocolate and ice-cream makers, and fabricators of crèche figures.

The selective survey of crafts that follows will make it easier for the reader to appreciate the richness and diversity that have always characterized the great family of *compagnonnage*.

Opposite: **Emblem representing the Trinity, dear to journeymen of the *devoir***

Carpenters (*Les Charpentiers*)

Under the Old Regime, the carpenters' guild long held sway over practitioners of other crafts, such as roofers, wheelwrights, and barrel makers. It lost its privileges in 1314, when the carpenters split into two subgroups: those of the *grande cognée*, or large ax (timber workers), and those of the *petite cognée*, or small ax (joiners). The first journeyman carpenters placed themselves under the authority of Father Soubise. During the French Revolution, many carpenters broke away to establish the *devoir de liberté*, and for

Joseph, the patron saint of journeyman carpenters, is duly celebrated by them every March 19. Whether journeyman carpenters focus on traditional carpentry or choose to specialize in industrial work, plywood, molds for casting concrete, reinforcement work, or stair construction, those who complete their Tour de France have bright futures ahead of them.

more than a century these two groups, respectively children of Soubise and of Solomon, were sworn enemies.

On November 25, 1945, the two rival groups merged to form the journeyman carpenters of the Devoirs du Tour de France. After countless disagreements, the new organization merged with the Fédération Compagnonnique des Métiers du Bâtiment, created in the 1950s. Note, however, that the rite of Soubise is still practiced within the Association Ouvrière after a few journeyman carpenters refused to accept the merger of 1945. Saint

Top: **Étienne Leclair, souvenir Tour-de-France drawing of *Périgord la Fidélité* (The Faithful One from Périgord), journeyman carpenter of the *devoir*, Edeline collection**

Left: **Walnut ornamental frame, a carpentry "masterpiece," 41½" h.**

Above: **Image commemorating awards presented to journeyman carpenters for their "masterpieces." The *indiens* and the *soubises* each had their own version of such awards.**

Joiners (*Les Menuisiers*)

In the sixteenth century, when they became workers of the "small ax," carpenters specializing in small-scale work became independent of the carpenters. They were long affiliated with *huissiers* (door makers), *lambrisseurs* (veneer specialists), *huchiers* (chest makers), and *châssiers* (specialists in window frames), the joiners' true ancestors. Their apprenticeships lasted six years.

Because she had given birth to the Virgin Mary, Saint Anne, the "tabernacle of God," was chosen as the patron saint of the joiners' guild. The journeyman joiners of the *devoir*, children of Master Jacques, date the founding of the confraternity to A.D. 570. In the seventeenth century, groups of dissident journeyman joiners broke away and declared themselves *non du devoir* (not of the *devoir*). Historically, this split originated in the revocation of the Edict of Nantes in 1685. After this

division, Catholic and Protestant journeyman joiners would be bitter rivals. Toward the end of the eighteenth century, the dissident *pays* opted to become affiliated with the *devoir de liberté*. To accentuate their difference from the *devoirants*, they declared themselves children of Solomon, and they soon came to be known as *gavots*.

The rivalry between *gavots* and *devoirants* was long-lived. A popular French television miniseries *Ardéchois Coeur Fidèle* (The Faithful Heart from Ardèche) was largely inspired by the brawls between these rival factions of journeyman joiners. The Montpellier competition (1803) is one of the most famous contests for a city monopoly in the history of the Tour de France. The *devoirants* are proud to count among them François Roux (1809–1865), known as *François le Champagne* (François from

Champagne), a truly gifted artist. The *gavots* also venerate *Avignonnais la Vertu* (The Virtuous One from Avignon), Agricol Perdiguier, the great nineteenth-century renewer and pacifier of *compagnonnage*.

Today, journeyman joiners of the *devoir* belong to the Association Ouvrière des Compagnons de Devoir du Tour de France, while the *gavots* are members of the Fédération Compagnonnique des Métiers du Bâtiment. In addition, a few joiners belong to the Union Compagnonnique des Devoirs Unis.

Left: **Sash of a *gavot* dignitary, 1859**

Nineteenth-century journeyman joiner of the *devoir de liberté* in mourning garb

Furniture Makers (*Les Ébénistes*)

The earliest known use of "*ébéniste*" dates from 1743. In the guilds of the Old Regime, the *ébénistes* (long known as *huchiers*, or chest makers and sculptors) always modeled their statutes after those of the *menuisiers* (joiners). They did the same in *compagnonnage*, where the two crafts were long confounded. In 1973, the Association Ouvrière des Compagnons du Devoir du Tour de France defined journeyman *ébénistes* in a way intended to distinguish them once and for all from journeyman joiners: "Journeymen *ébénistes* should be capable of conceiving and realizing pieces of furniture that are rectangular or bulging, solid or veneered, contemporary or historical in style, consistent with accepted craft practices." *Ébénistes* maintain ties with other professionals such as decorators, upholsterers, painters, lacquer specialists, marble craftsmen, and wood

carvers, and so are able to develop any number of specialties (contemporary furniture, period furniture, etc.). In the Fédération Compagnonnique des Métiers du Bâtiment, under the aegis of the *devoir de liberté*, journeyman furniture makers are still considered *gavots*. Among the latter, Alfred Samblancat, known as *Bigourdan le Corinthien* ("Bigourdan from Corinthe"), who worked in an emphatically

Above: **Saint Anne, patron saint of journeyman joiners and furniture makers**

Left: **Miniature Louis XV sofa with sinuous frame and openwork "net" seat, all made of wood, 4½″ h. This "masterpiece" was made in Montpellier about 1850.**

futurist style, was nicknamed the "mad *ébéniste*" in the 1970s. All journeyman furniture makers honor Saint Anne.

Coopers (*Les Tonneliers-Doleurs*)

Barrel makers long belonged to the same guild as carpenters. Sometimes called *charpentiers en tonneaux* (barrel carpenters), they obtained a guild of their own in 1376. They were also known as *doleurs* after the *doloire*, a heavy ax they used to cut the staves of their flasks and barrels. Generally, their apprenticeship lasted five years.

The first journeyman confraternity of coopers was established in 1702 or 1722. Children of Master Jacques, they honor John the Baptist as their patron saint. In the early decades of the nineteenth century, an organization of journeyman coopers was established, affiliated with the *devoir de liberté* who were children of Solomon, but it no longer exists.

Until the first decades of the twentieth century, journeyman coopers of the *devoir* had a special relationship with the Dominicans and Franciscans, who welcomed them in their monasteries along the Tour de France. Using the *doloire*, they made a lengthwise incision in their left thumb, leaving a scar that signified their membership in the *devoir*. The most important cities on their Tour de France were Beaune, Cognac, and Tours.

The nineteenth-century journeyman Patrice, known as *Angoumois l'Ami des Arts* (The Friend of the Arts from Angoulême), remains the champion of this organization, for the superb craftsmanship of his productions has never been surpassed. Several of his works are on display in the Museum of Compagnonnage in Tours.

Above: **The *doloire*, or heavy ax, used by journeyman coopers of the *devoir*, Museum of Compagnonnage, Tours**

Left: **Miniature barrels incorporating marquetry work by the journeyman Raymond Besnard, known as *Blois l'Ami du Trait*, or The Friend of the *Trait* from Blois, Museum of Compagnonnage, Tours**

Woodturners (*Les Tourneurs sur Bois*)

Master Jacques, the journeyman turners of the *devoir* honored Saint Michael. They disappeared early in the twentieth century, but the Union Compagnonnique des Devoirs Unis is trying to reinvigorate their traditions by accepting a few journeymen interested in reviving this singular craft.

Left: **Saint Michael, patron saint of journeyman woodturners**

Below: **As their "masterpieces," journeyman woodturners often make delicate "tremblers" out of boxwood, whose narrow stems are punctuated by rings and other distinctive shapes.**

Originally members of the carpenters' guild, woodturners obtained statutes of their own in the fifteenth century (1467). Their apprenticeship lasted four years. Working with boxwood, maple, and tortoiseshell, they made distaffs, bowls, and ladders, as well as the billiard balls made of ivory for which they were famous. They also fashioned spinning wheels, wig stands, and artificial arms and legs in wartime. They entered the world of *compagnonnage* in 1700, or, according to an alternative account, in 1643 in Nantes, where they were sponsored by the journeyman carpenters of the *devoir*. As children of

Wheelwrights (*Les Charrons*) and *Carrossiers*

Long under the authority of the carpenters' guild, wheelwrights obtained their own statutes in the fifteenth century (1467). Their newfound independence prompted them to select a new protector, and Saint Joseph was abandoned for Saint Catherine. Her martyrdom on the wheel made her a singularly appropriate choice, and she had not been adopted by any other craft.

The wheelwrights entered the journeyman world in Bordeaux in 1638, thanks to their recognition by the journeyman *tail-lendiers* (edge-tool makers) of the *devoir* in that city. An alternative account places their entry somewhat later, in 1706. They have a special veneration for Ferdinand Flouret (1851–1939), whose "masterpieces" are now in the collection of the Conservatoire National des Arts et Métiers, which has lent some of them to the Museum of Compagnonnage in Tours. After the

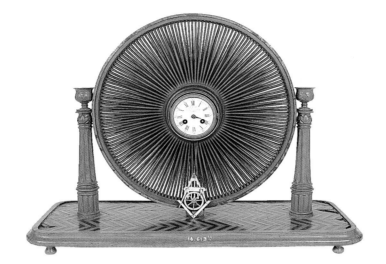

Left: **Extraordinary wheel with 504 spokes made by Ferdinand Flouret (1851–1939), known as *Dauphiné la Bonne Espérance* (The Great Hope of Dauphiné)**

Below: **The wheelwrights managed to adapt their skills to the new demands presented by the automobile.**

introduction of the automobile, the journeyman wheelwrights transformed themselves into the journeyman wheelwrights and *carrossiers* (automobile body makers) of the *devoir*, an adaptive move that proved completely successful.

In our day, these craftsmen, affiliated with the Association Ouvrière, enjoy considerable prestige. Large automobile manufacturers hire them to work up

important new designs. Renault Industrial Vehicles, for example, engaged journeyman *carrossiers* of the *devoir* to assist in the development of their industrial heavy-vehicle line known by the acronym VIRAGES (Véhicule Industriel de Recherche Améliorant le Gestion de l'Énergie et de la Sécurité). Journeyman *carrossiers* of the *devoir* still revere Saint Catherine.

Sabot Makers (*Les Sabotiers*)

Imaginative *sabots*, made of walnut and beech, fashioned by the
journeyman Olivier, whose work
can be seen at the Museum of
Compagnonnage in Tours

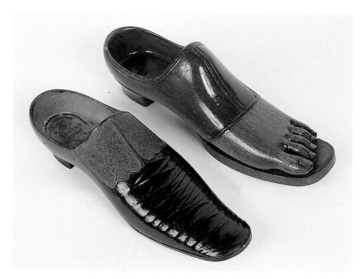

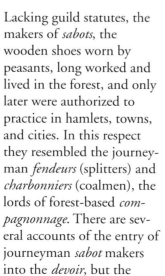

Lacking guild statutes, the makers of *sabots*, the wooden shoes worn by peasants, long worked and lived in the forest, and only later were authorized to practice in hamlets, towns, and cities. In this respect they resembled the journey-man *fendeurs* (splitters) and *charbonniers* (coalmen), the lords of forest-based *com-pagnonnage*. There are sev-eral accounts of the entry of journeyman *sabot* makers into the *devoir*, but the most widely accepted dates

the event to 1809. In real-ity, they were not officially recognized until 1850 or 1865 (even here, accounts differ). Their patron saint was Saint René. The last of the journeyman *sabot* mak-ers decided to become affili-ated with the naissant Union Compagnonnique. Among the most eminent of their members are the two *pays* Gautier and Olivier, whose work still compels the admiration of visitors to the Museum of Compagnonnage in Tours.

Stonecutters (*Les Tailleurs de Pierre*)

According to the *Livre des métiers* (Book of crafts) published in 1268 under the authority of Étienne Boileau, *entailleurs de pierre* and *espilleurs*, as these craftsmen were then known, were a branch of the masons, whose statutes they shared. This meant that they were under the authority of the overseers of the king of France. In general, their apprenticeships lasted seven years.

The craft has adopted several patron saints, notably Blaise, Peter, Roch, Thomas, and Reinhold, the latter probably a corruption of Renaud of Montauban, one of the four sons of Aymon that figure in a medieval *chanson de geste* (song of exploits) dear to

journeyman stonecutters. The great Germanic lodges venerate the "four crowned ones," who likewise figure in the symbolism of French journeyman stonecutters.

The *étrangers* stonecutters, children of Solomon known as *loups*, are reputedly the oldest of all journeymen, for which reason they always appear at the top of the journeyman hierarchy. These *étrangers*, who later rallied behind the flag of the *devoir de liberté*, disappeared in the early decades of the twentieth century, despite an attempt at revival initiated in 1923 by Albert Bernet, known as

Above: **Maquette of a kiosk, a *chef-d'oeuvre de prestige*, or prestige masterpiece, made in the early twentieth century by the journeyman Leturgeon, known as *La Fidélité de Vouvray* (The Faithful One from Vouvray), approx. 39″ h. In 1968, it was restored by the journeyman Chardonneau, known as *L'Amitié de Châteaurenard* (The Friendly One from Châteaurenard).**

Left: **A stonecutter finishing the step of a spiral stair**

La Liberté de Séméac (The Liberated One from Séméac). Marseilles and Paris were the last cities where the *loups* had *mères*.

Stonecutters

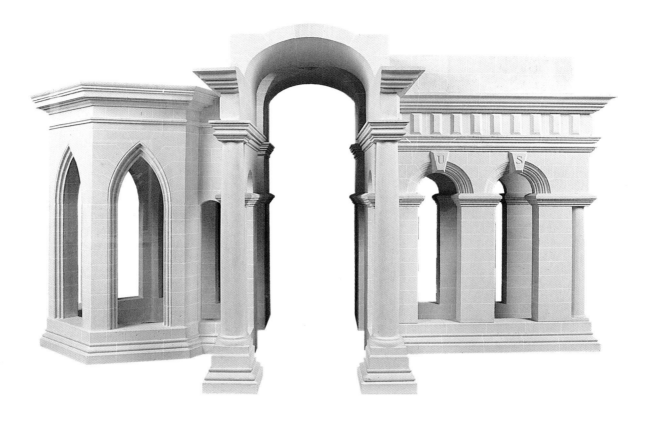

Above: **Reception masterpiece in the form of a diminutive temple, made in 1965 by the journeyman Robert Noyers, known as** *Angevin la Persévérance de Ménil* **(The Perseverance of Ménil from Angers), approx. 4¼' h. Note the inclusion of both pointed Gothic arches (left) and rounded arches (right).**

Right: **Maquette of the ribbing of a Gothic vault, made by the journeyman of the** *devoir* **Serge Laisney, known as** *La Fraternité de Geffosses* **(The Fraternal One from Geffosses), less than 19" h.**

Itinerant journeyman stonecutters of the *devoir*, known as *loups-garous*, children of Master Jacques, also lay claim to an early origin (558 B.C.). For more than two centuries, they quarreled bitterly with the *loups*. Aside from the brawls in Lunel (1816) and Nantes (1825), the tragic episode in Tournus (1825–26) remains the most notorious battle between these fraternal enemies. Presently, itinerant journeyman stonecutters of the *devoir* belong to the Association Ouvrière des Compagnons du Devoir du Tour de France. Journeyman *maçons-tailleurs*, or mason-stone dressers, of the *devoir*, who are affiliated with the Fédération Compagnon-nique des Métiers du Bâtiment, claim the heritage of the *étrangers* as their own. This venerable group of craftsmen places itself under the protection of none other than the Ascension, for legend has it that masons and stonecutters helped Christ escape from the tomb by loosening the heavy stone that blocked its entry.

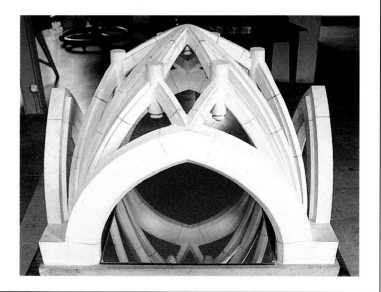

Roofers (*Les Couvreurs*)

In the thirteenth-century *Livre des métiers,* roofers are listed as being under the supervision of the carpenters. They obtained statutes of their own early in the fourteenth century, when apprenticeships lasted four years. In the eighteenth century, this training was extended to six years. Because the profession was so dangerous, masters were prohibited from allowing their apprentices to work alone on rooftops until they had received three years of training in the masters' presence. Known for their agility and

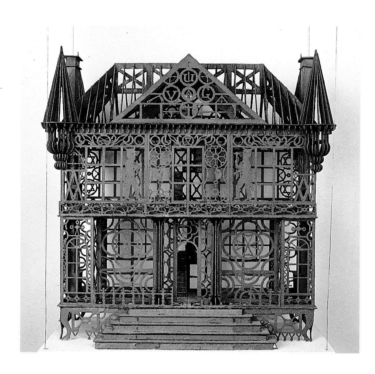

Left: **Small manor house made entirely of slate by *France Va de Bon Coeur* (The Stalwart One from France), approx. 20″ h.**

Below: **Print celebrating the craft of roofing, 1848**

Bottom left: **Large "masterpiece" by the journeyman Bonvous**

courage, the roofers of earlier days were known as *chats* (cats) or, more often, as *coucous* (cuckoos).

Itinerant journeyman roofers of the *devoir*, children of Father Soubise known as *bons drilles* (good fellows), were first welcomed into the world of *compagnonnage* in 1759. An alternative account holds that this event took place in 1703, thanks to the sponsorship of journeyman carpenters of the rite of Soubise. Given that every region of France had its own characteristic roof treatments, the Tour de France served this craft particularly well, producing artisans of remarkable versatility.

Among the most famous roofers, we should certainly mention Auguste Bonvous, known as *Angevin la Fidélité le*

Soutien du Devoir (The Faithful Stay of the *Devoir* from Angers), who, early in the twentieth century, was already envisioning a reinvigorated *compagnonnage.* His innovative ideas won him the nickname "the intellectual of *compagnonnage.*" Today, most journeyman roofers belong either

to the Association Ouvrière des Compagnons du Devoir or to the Fédération Compagnonnique des Métiers du Bâtiment. The *zingueurs*, or zinc-workers, belong to the same journeyman organization as the roofers. All of them celebrate the feast day of the Ascension.

Plaster Workers (*Les Plâtriers*)

Two plaster workers of the
Association Ouvrière des
Compagnons du Devoir du Tour
de France

It is sometimes said that the first journeyman plaster workers received the *devoir* in 1703, due to the sponsorship of the journeyman carpenters, children of Father Soubise. In fact, they were officially recognized by Tour-de-France journeymen only in 1797. Today there are journeyman plasterers on the rolls of all three journeyman organizations, but the great majority of them belong to the Association Ouvrière des Compagnons du Devoir.

The natural material gypsum becomes plaster or stucco when it is dehydrated. When ground into a powder and mixed with water, the result is a malleable substance easy to fashion into any number of shapes and designs, or made to resemble marble or stone. In some cases, the elements of an ensemble are made in the workshop by craftsmen and subsequently assembled on site, where the plastering of walls remains the craft's fundamental skill.

Locksmiths (*Les Serruriers*)

In the Middle Ages, the most prestigious activity of iron locksmiths was the fabrication of doors for cathedrals, castles, and châteaus. The *Livre des métiers* cites an important law intended to keep order in the realm: Make no key without having the lock in front of your eyes! The locksmiths' guild was subject to an exceptional degree of surveillance, but there were compensations,

for keymakers were greatly esteemed.

Journeyman locksmiths of the *devoir*, children of Master Jacques, date their origins to A.D. 570. After the revocation of the Edict of Nantes (1685), disagreements led to the establishment of dissident groups affiliated with the *devoir de liberté* (initially known as *non du devoir*). They shared *mères* with the journeyman joiners of the *devoir de lib-*

Examples of elaborate, antique locks

erté and, like them, were known as *gavots*.

As with the journeyman joiners, *devoirants* and *gavots* locksmiths quarreled frequently. In 1807, a competition was organized between them for the craft monopoly in Marseilles. The formidable lock shaped like a cross of the Légion d'Honneur fashioned by the competitor representing the *devoirants* won them craft control in the city for no less than a hundred years. Saint Peter replaced Saint Éloi as the patron saint of journeyman locksmiths of the *devoir de*

liberté, who, as worthy *gavots*, also venerate Saint Anne.

Currently the Association Ouvrière des Compagnons du Devoir du Tour de France is the organizational home of all journeyman locksmiths of the *devoir* professing the rite of Master Jacques. Increasingly, the latter are replacing the term *"serrurier,"* or locksmith, with the more modern *"métallier,"* or metalworker. They take particular pride in having helped fashion a new flaming torch for the Statue of Liberty in New

York on the occasion of its centennial in 1986.

Journeyman locksmiths of the *devoir de liberté*, inseparable from the joiners of the same rite, have joined the Fédération Compagnonnique des Métiers du Bâtiment. The profession entails work with aluminum and wrought iron, metallic construction, locksmithing, and interior decoration.

Glaziers (*Les Vitriers*)

On cathedral construction sites, the guild of master glaziers enjoyed considerable prestige. Guardians of the secrets of their craft, they produced splendid stained-glass windows, such as those at Chartres, that still compel the admiration of connoisseurs.

Glaziers were accepted into *compagnonnage* at the very beginning of the eighteenth century. The first journeyman glaziers were sponsored by the journeyman locksmiths of the *devoir* and thus expanded the group of the children of Master Jacques. Being worthy *chiens* (dogs), they did not hesitate to howl during their ritual ceremonies.

The oldest known account of journeyman cul-ture was written by a journeyman glazier of the *devoir*, Jacques Ménétra, known as *Parisien le Bienvenu* (The Welcome Parisian), and is titled *Journal of My Life,* the original manuscript of which is in the Bibliothèque Historique de la Ville de Paris. The organization of journeyman glaziers of the *devoir* flourished during the eighteenth century but then gradually declined. Saint Luke is the patron saint of this craft, in which the symbolism of light has played a uniquely important role. Currently, the Union Compagnonnique des Devoirs Unis is the only organization that accepts journeyman glaziers.

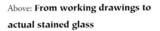
Above: **From working drawings to actual stained glass**

Left: **Alain Poisson, journeyman glazier of the Devoirs Unis, known as *Parisien l'Harmonie de la Lumière* (The Harmony of Light from Paris)**

Farriers (*Les Maréchaux-Ferrants*)

In the *Livre des métiers*, the guild of the farriers is said to be under the authority of the First Marshal of the Stables of the King of France. For many centuries, these craftsmen not only shoed horses but also served as the only veterinarians.

Journeyman farriers of the *devoir*, children of Master Jacques and sometimes referred to as *chiens noirs* (black dogs), were recognized in Lyon in 1789 with the support of the journeyman blacksmiths, who had been received into the *devoir* in 1609. Other archival documents date the farriers' reception to 1795 or even as late as

Tour de France (The muses of the Tour de France). In the nineteenth century, the journeyman farriers were among the most powerful groups on the Tour. Since horses were replaced by mechanized transport, very few farriers remain in the three journeyman organizations. However, more and more youngsters are eager to learn from them, so the organization of journeyman farriers of the *devoir* has not yet disappeared from the landscape of *compagnonnage*.

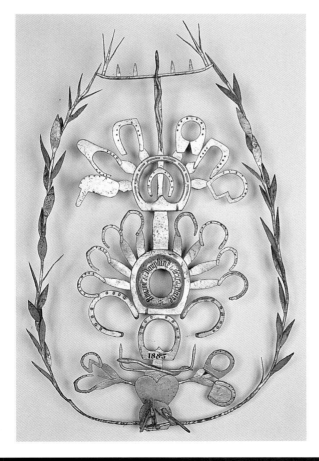

1867. Like the practitioners of most iron crafts, journeyman farriers venerate Saint Éloi. Accordingly, the "masterpiece sign" that journeyman farriers placed outside their workshops were dubbed "bouquets of Saint Éloi." Journeymen incorporated the full range of horseshoes they could forge or apply into these "bouquets," which reflected the breadth of the experience they had acquired on the Tour de France.

Among the most famous practitioners of this craft is Abel Boyer (1882–1959), known as *Périgord Coeur Loyal* (The Loyal Heart from Périgord), the writer and poet who in 1925–26 masterminded the encyclopedia *Les Muses du*

Above: **François Bernadet, known as *Toulousain le Bien Aimé* (The Well-Loved One from Toulouse), flanked by two of his prestige masterpieces**

Left: **A "bouquet of Saint Éloi," reception piece of the journeyman farrier Bouzon, known as *Dauphiné le Désir de Plaire* (The One Eager to Please from Dauphiné), 1883**

Workers of Lead and Zinc (*Les Pombiers-Zingueurs*)

In the guild system of the Old Regime, lead workers were subsidiary members of the roofers' guild. In the later Middle Ages, they gained a certain prominence by laying down sheets of lead over the roofs of many churches, cathedrals, and châteaus. They also added decorative elements to roofs in the form of crowning grilles and other objects. There was less demand for these delicate ornaments beginning in the early sixteenth century. In *compagnonnage*, journeyman workers of lead and zinc are grouped with

journeyman roofers, with whom they share a particular veneration for the feast of the Ascension. Currently, practitioners of this craft are accepted by all three journeyman organizations. Also worth mentioning is the proliferation of *plombiers-chauffagistes* (specialists in heating and plumbing systems), who are especially numerous in the journeyman organizations.

Above: **Miniature bathroom installation made of lead, zinc, copper, and brass, 1890, Edeline collection**

Left: **Bust of David, reception piece presented in 1975 by J. P. Rurgoat, known as *Breton la Persévérance* (The Persistent One from Brittany), journeyman lead worker of the Devoirs Unis**

Makers of Shoes and Boots
(*Les Cordonniers-Bottiers*)

Makers of shoes and boots came to be known as *cordouaniers* because for quite some time the finest treated goatskin came from Cordova (Cordoue in French). These craftsmen later obtained their leather from Morocco, which led to the coining of the French term *"maroquinerie"* (goods made of Morocco leather). The revised version of the guild statutes in the *Livre des métiers* specifies an apprenticeship of four years.

The craft was not recognized by the journeyman world until 1807, an acceptance granted official status in 1850. There must have been journeyman practitioners of the craft much earlier, for it is mentioned in religious condemnations of the confraternity of the Très Saint-Sacrement de l'Autel (Very Holy Sacrament of the Altar), notably one issued by the Sorbonne in

leather family of the Association Ouvrière des Compagnons du Devoir, within the framework of the organization of journeyman saddlers, shoe makers, and boot makers of the *devoir* on the Tour de France.

Left: **Saints Crispin and Crispinian, the patron saints of shoe and boot makers**

Bottom left: **"Louis XV" boot made in 1879 by the journeyman Pinet**

Bottom right: **Bootery "masterpieces" by Pierre Capus, known as** *Albigeois l'Ami des Arts* **(The Friend of the Arts from Albi), 1850**

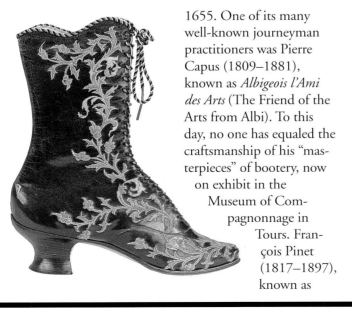

1655. One of its many well-known journeyman practitioners was Pierre Capus (1809–1881), known as *Albigeois l'Ami des Arts* (The Friend of the Arts from Albi). To this day, no one has equaled the craftsmanship of his "masterpieces" of bootery, now on exhibit in the Museum of Compagnonnage in Tours. François Pinet (1817–1897), known as

Tourangeau la Rose d'Amour (The Rose of Love from Touraine), also brought renown to his craft, boasting clients for his boots throughout the world.

Journeyman makers of shoes and boots of the *devoir* have always honored Saints Crispin and Crispinian as their patrons. At the end of the nineteenth century, many of them joined the Union Compagnonnique des Devoirs Unis. Today, they have regrouped in the

Makers of Harnesses, Saddles, and Bridles
(*Les Bourreliers-Selliers-Harnacheurs*)

Although subsidiary to the saddlers' guild, the makers of harnesses and bridles had their own statutes in the thirteenth century. The *Livre des métiers* specifies that apprenticeships were to last four years. Harness makers were accepted as journeymen starting in 1687, a status officially confirmed in 1706. As for saddle makers, they entered the journeyman fold in 1702. With the advent of the automobile, these craftsmen, like the journeyman wheelwrights, had to adapt by developing new skills. Currently, they are among the best makers and upholsterers of automobile seats, and are making inroads into airplane seating as well.

Furthermore, they are learning to use new technology such as laser-cutters to cut and treat material. The founder and first president of the Union Compagnonnique des Devoirs Unis was a journeyman harness and bridle maker of the *devoir*, Lucien Blanc (1823–1909), known as *Provençal le Résolu* (The Resolute One from Provence).

Since World War II, most members of this craft group have joined the leather family of the Association Ouvrière des Compagnons du Devoir du Tour de France. They honor Saints Crispin and Crispinian.

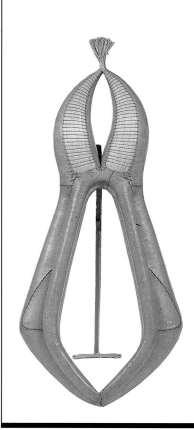

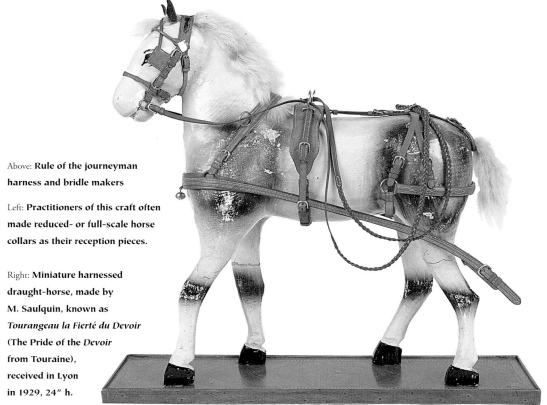

Above: **Rule of the journeyman harness and bridle makers**

Left: **Practitioners of this craft often made reduced- or full-scale horse collars as their reception pieces.**

Right: **Miniature harnessed draught-horse, made by M. Saulquin, known as *Tourangeau la Fierté du Devoir* (The Pride of the *Devoir* from Touraine), received in Lyon in 1929, 24″ h.**

Basket Makers (*Les Vanniers*)

The earliest known statutes for a basket makers' guild date from the fifteenth century. The apprenticeship for this craft was not very long. In general, three years sufficed to master the arts of plaiting and basket making. The descendants of rural craftsmen, the earliest basket makers placed their guild under the protection of Saint Anthony, for tradition holds that this hermit passed the time by plaiting palm and willow leaves.

There are two accounts of the establishment of this craft body in journeyman tradition. The first holds that the body of journeyman basket makers of the *devoir*, children of Master Jacques, was established in 1409. According to the sec-

ond, these craftsmen were accepted by the journeyman community only in 1788. The craft group, whose patron saint was Saint Anthony, gradually disappeared in the nineteenth century.

Nonetheless, we should mention the work of Sylvian Dupont, known as *Tourangeau la Corbeille d'Amour* (The Basket of Love from Touraine), who several years ago attempted to revive the traditions and skills associated with this craft, which reached its apogee in the eighteenth century. Like many other venerable crafts, this one was unable to maintain its place within the journeyman family.

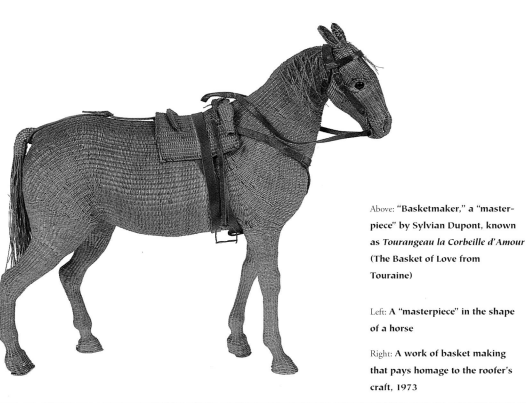

Above: **"Basketmaker," a "masterpiece" by Sylvian Dupont, known as *Tourangeau la Corbeille d'Amour* (The Basket of Love from Touraine)**

Left: **A "masterpiece" in the shape of a horse**

Right: **A work of basket making that pays homage to the roofer's craft, 1973**

Rope Makers (*Les Cordiers*)

Thanks to the *Livre des métiers,* we know that by 1268 the rope makers' guild had statutes of its own. Apprenticeships lasted four years. In return for supplying hemp rope for use in the execution of the king's justice, rope makers were exempt from paying taxes.

It is said that rope makers began to enter the journeyman world as early as 1407. However, this craft was not officially accepted until 1735, under the sponsorship of the journeyman harness makers of the *devoir* in the city of Marseilles. Journeyman rope makers knew their true moment of glory in the days of the tall ships. This explains the frequent location of their chapter houses within naval dockyards, as in Toulon.

Journeyman rope makers possessed craft secrets that made it possible for them to produce magnificent plaited cord and extraordinary "endless rings." Candidates for the title of journeyman had to be able to make these rings, which entailed plaiting hemp cord around an iron ring such that no seams or ends could be detected. Among the most famous members of this journeyman organization, which is no longer extant, was the *pays* Louis Barthès, known as *Plein d'Honneur le Languedocien* (The One Full of Honor from Languedoc), who produced several impressive "masterpieces," some of which are exhibited at the Museum of Compagnonnage in Tours. Paul Calas, known as *L'Ami des Filles le Languedocien* (The Friend to Girls from Languedoc), became famous in the second half of the nineteenth century for his songs, several of which are still hummed on the Tour de France. Journeyman rope makers of the *devoir* honored Saint Paul, Saint Severin, and, above all, Saint Peter of the Chains.

Top: **Large "masterpiece" of hemp plaiting celebrating the three founding fathers of *compagnonnage*, approx. 4' h. Within the "pediment," a photograph of its maker, Louis Barthès, known as *Plein d'Honneur le Languedocien* (The One Full of Honor from Languedoc)**

Left: **Large "endless ring" whose hemp cord is more than three inches thick**

Dyers (*Les Teinturiers*)

The dyers' guild was very powerful in the Middle Ages. It is said that the first dyers were received as journeymen in 1330, but there is no documentation to support this claim. As children of Master Jacques, journeyman dyers of the *devoir* wore, in addition to their colors, a symbolic rectangular apron made of crimson wool. The common and symbolic names of the dyer were embroidered on the apron along with the device: "God protect journeymen of the *devoir.*" As another feature specific to journeyman dyers, the great majority of them were received in Lyon, their craft's "mother" city on the Tour de France. Fervent Catholics, they disappeared early in the twentieth century, after many of the last journeyman dyers joined the Union Compagnonnique des Devoirs Unis.

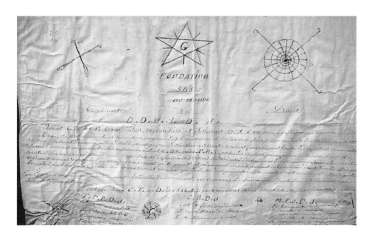

Above: **Apron of a journeyman dyer of the *devoir*, Museum of Compagnonnage, Tours**

Left: **A nineteenth-century forgery of the founding document of the confraternity of dyers, on parchment (original document c. A.D. 548), Museum of Compagnonnage, Tours**

Leather Bleachers and Dressers
(*Les Blanchers-Chamoiseurs*)

The term *"blancher"* appeared at the end of the fourteenth century, replacing the word *"mégissier"* (leather dresser). These craftsmen bleached the skins of sheep and goats to make supple the kidskin or chamois used to make gloves. *Chamoiseurs* treated chamois, the flesh side of sheepskin, after it had been tanned with oil.

Tradition holds that leather dressers were received as journeymen in 1370, in the city of Orléans. In 1500, they joined forces with the leather bleachers to establish a common journeyman confraternity. In 1840, its elders asked Jean-François Piron (1796–1841), known as *Vendôme la Clef des Coeurs* (The Key of Hearts from Vendôme), to draft new statutes, which were published in Paris under the title *Le Devoir des compagnons blanchers et chamoiseurs réunis* (The *devoir* of the united journeyman leather bleachers and leather dressers). *Vendôme la Clef des Coeurs* was also a celebrated songwriter who placed his talent and renown entirely at the service of Agricol Perdiguier's project of reform.

The organization accepted only Catholic craftsmen, and all foreigners were also refused. These journeymen, children of Master Jacques, regarded the pilgrimage to Sainte-Baume as a sacred obligation. They honored Mary

Left: **Portrait of Jean-François Piron, known as *Vendôme la Clef des Coeurs* (The Key of Hearts from Vendôme)**

Below: **Print depicting journeyman leather bleacher and dresser making his pilgrimage to Sainte-Baume, nineteenth century**

Magdalene, Saint Germain of Auxerre, and Saint John the Baptist, for he wore animal skins. By the late nineteenth century they had only two chapters on the Tour de France, Paris and Grenoble.

Weavers and Cloth Makers (*Les Tisseurs-Ferrandiniers*)

Originally known as *teciers* or *tissiers de toile* (cloth weavers), these craftsmen obtained their own guild statutes in the fifteenth century. Their apprenticeships lasted five years. The second word in their hyphenated French name derives from *ferrandine*, a light cloth invented in the seventeenth century by a resident of Lyon whose last name was Ferrand.

Weavers were first accepted as journeymen in 1834, and their craft officially entered *compagnonnage* ten years later under the sponsorship of the journeyman saddlers of Lyon. Some journeyman weavers wore earrings from which they hung miniatures of the tools used in their profession. In the nineteenth century, they produced magnificent portraits that are veritable masterpieces of weaving. Unfortunately, this confraternity disappeared early in the twentieth century, a victim of the introduction of mechanical weaving.

We are indebted to the journeyman weavers for the famous song *Les Fils de la vierge* (The sons of the Virgin), which is still sung during the ritual known as the Chain of Alliance. One of the most famous members of this organization was the *pays* Galibert, known as *Dauphiné la Clef des Coeurs* (The Key of Hearts from Dauphiné), a songwriter well known on the Tour de France who actively supported

Perdiguier's project to reconcile and unify the various journeyman confraternities.

Above: **Portrait of Jacquard, silk, 3' h., woven by journeyman weavers of the *devoir* in 1839**

Right: **Journeyman weaver in the ceremonial dress of a *rouleur*, early nineteenth century**

Hatters (*Les Chapeliers*)

The hat makers' guild is mentioned in the *Livre des métiers*, and tradition holds that the craft was accepted into *compagnonnage* in 1410, although there is no historical proof of this. In the eighteenth century, journeyman hat makers and nail makers were sworn enemies. Whenever they encountered one another on the roads of the Tour de France, brawls ensued.

This confraternity underwent a remarkable transformation in 1872, when the journeyman Bouchard, known as *La Prudence le Bourguignon* (The Prudent One from Burgundy), newly returned from a thirty-year stint in Africa, undertook a campaign of reform. After taking stock of his organization's sorry state, he resolved to breathe new life into it. He visited all of its chapters on the Tour de

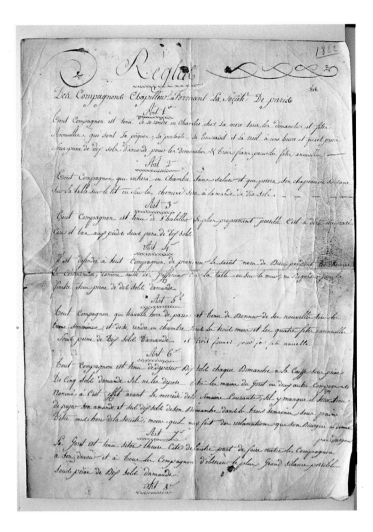

France and convinced them to accept *approprieurs* into their ranks. These workers, whose name derives from *propre* ("clean"), were responsible for cleaning hats and making them fit for sale after they had been fashioned by the *fouleurs* (from *fouler*, "to press"). Although they had always been excluded from *compagnonnage*, their craft considered inferior by the *fouleurs,* the sudden admission of large numbers of these "cleaners" greatly increased the organization's size and power, introducing as well a new spirit of camaraderie.

The organization of the children of Master Jacques experienced a period of irreversible decline in the early years of the twentieth century, mechanization having rendered its members' skills obsolete.

Above: **Rule of the Parisian chapter of the journeyman hatters of the** *devoir*

Left: **Pommel of the staff of a journeyman hatter of the** *devoir*

Bakers (*Les Boulangers*)

Above: **Coat of arms of the journeyman bakers of the *devoir* fashioned from bread dough**

Right: ***Parisienne la Bien Aimée* (The Well-Loved Parisian)**, *mère* of journeyman bakers of the *devoir*, 1924

Below: **Journeyman image celebrating the craft's devotion to Saint Honoré**

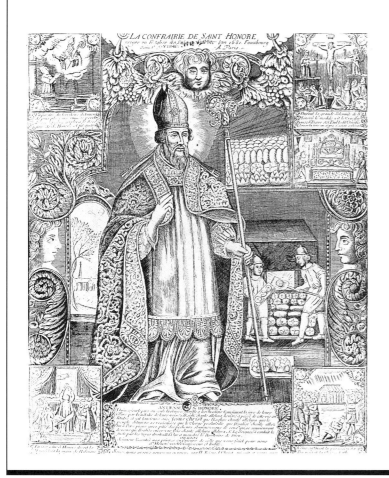

Known successively as *pistores talemeliers* (from the Latin *pistor*, "miller/baker") and then *boulangiers* (because bread was baked in the shape of a *boule*, or ball), French bread makers were called *boulangers* beginning in the sixteenth century. The first journeyman bakers were initiated in 1811 by a journeyman maker of barrels and casks known as *Bavarois Beau Désir* (The Ardent One from Bavaria). The latter, having fallen ill and been effectively abandoned by his fellow journeymen, was cared for by two bakers.

By way of thanks, *Bavarois Beau Désir* revealed to them the secrets of the *devoir*. Thus were created the first two journeyman bakers of the *devoir* of the Tour de France, who were given the symbolic names *Nivernais Frappe d'Abord* (Knock First from Nivernais) and *Montbard l'Inviolable* (The Inviolable One from Montbard). *Bavarois Beau Désir*, accused of having betrayed *compagnonnage*, fled to America to escape the violence threatened against him by the journeymen in his craft confraternity. Mockingly dubbed *soi-disant de la raclette* ("scraper-pretenders"), journeyman bakers had to endure many insults and indignities from the members of established journeyman confraternities who did not want to accept them. They were finally welcomed into the fold in 1860. It is worth noting that the organization of journeyman bakers of the *devoir* is one of very few to possess documentation of its entry into *compagnonnage*.

In the past, only a few journeyman bakers were received into the *devoir de liberté*. At present, the great majority of journeyman bakers belong to the Association Ouvrière, where they sponsored the entry of the journeyman pastry chefs of the *devoir*. The Union Compagnonnique also has a few bakers on its rolls. To qualify for reception as a journeyman baker, generally one must demonstrate the ability to make several different kinds of bread (rye bread, bran bread, nutbread, leavened bread, etc.) as well as an assortment of basic pastries. Journeyman bakers of the *devoir* have always celebrated the feast of Saint Honoré, who was a sixth-century Bishop of Amiens.

Pastry Chefs (*Les Pâtissiers*)

In the thirteenth century, pastry makers belonged to the guild of *pastillarii* (from the Latin *pastillum*, "sacrificial cake"). In 1440, when they obtained guild statutes of their own, they became known as *pastissiers*. Pastry chefs have been accepted into *compagnonnage* for several decades now thanks to the sponsorship of the journeyman bakers, with whom they constitute a subsection of the Association Ouvrière. The Union Compagnonnique also accepts pastry chefs, but not the Fédération Compagnonnique, which admits only those in the building trades. To be received as a journeyman pastry chef, one must present a piece of work demonstrating mastery of the profession's various aspects: French pastry, chocolate, confectionaries, and ice cream as well as decoration and the special skills required of pastry caterers. Journeyman pastry chefs celebrate Saint Honoré.

Saint Honoré.

Left: **Journeyman image celebrating Saint Honoré**

Below: **A work by a journeyman pastry chef**

Cooks (*Les Cuisiniers*)

The *Livre des métiers* refers to master *queux* (from the Latin *coquus*, "cook") who sold boiled and roast meat. Gradually, the thirteenth-century *coquinarii* evolved into what we now call cooks. Of the three journeyman organizations, only the Union Compagnonnique admits journeyman cooks. Their official acceptance dates to 1912, when their first chapter was established in Paris. Since the celebrated Escoffier, many of the great names of French cuisine have worn the red sash of the Union Compagnonnique. The reputation of journeyman cooks of the Devoirs Unis extends well beyond the borders of France.

Above: **Model of the Hôtel-Dieu in Beaune made by *Bourguignon le Disciple de la Sainte-Baume* (The Disciple of Sainte-Baume from Burgundy), journeyman cook of the Devoirs Unis. Incorporating some forty-four pounds of noodle pastry, the model is the result of eight hundred hours of work.**

Glossary

This glossary of terms, many in French, is meant to facilitate the reader's access to a specialized vocabulary that can be confusing and sometimes even forbidding. Only terms relating to the text of this book are included, and definitions have been kept as brief as possible.

Adoption: Ceremony marking a young man's intention to complete the Tour de France

Affiliation: Ceremony marking a young man's affiliation with the *devoir de liberté*

Affilié (affiliate): An aspirant in the *devoir de liberté*

Ancien (elder): A journeyman who plays an important role in induction ceremonies (receptions); a journeyman who has satisfied all requirements for full membership in a journeyman organization; a retired journeyman

Aspirant: A young man adopted by a journeyman organization in order to complete his Tour de France

Assembly: Gathering of all journeymen to deliberate questions relative to the chapter or organization

Bons drilles (good fellows): Nickname for journeymen professing the rite of Father Soubise

Brûleur (burner): An aspirant or journeyman who has left a city without settling his debts and/or satisfying his obligations. He is blackballed from all chapters of the Tour de France

Carré: Journeyman passport that follows the itinerant throughout his Tour de France and is stamped in each city that he visits

Cayenne: Journeyman assembly site or a chapter house; the assemblies themselves

Chain of Alliance: Ritual ceremony performed at certain journeyman celebrations and sometimes at funerals. Wearing their colors, the journeymen form a circle, cross arms, and hold hands, like links in a chain. Two or three journeymen and the *mère* stand in the center of the circle, and the *rouleur* is called upon to sing

Chef-d'oeuvre ("masterpiece"): A work intended to demonstrate mastery of the basic skills of one's craft, or, in some cases, one's virtuosity. Anyone wishing to acquire the status of master in a craft guild, or of journeyman in a journeyman organization, is first obliged to present and have approved a "masterpiece"

Chien (dog): Nickname for journeyman *passant bons drilles* (itinerant good fellows)

Chien-loup (dog-wolf): Nickname for journeyman carpenters of the *devoirs* after the merger between the journeyman carpenters of the *devoir* (*chiens*) and those of the *devoir de liberté* (*loups* or *indiens*)

Children: All journeymen are the "children" of the founding fathers of their rite: Solomon, Master Jacques, or Father Soubise

Colors (*couleurs*): Silk or velvet ribbons and sashes bearing the emblems and symbols of one's journeyman organization. They vary in color and design according to one's craft and professed rite

Compagnon: Journeyman. In the hierarchy of the guilds, a professional status between apprentice and master; a craftsperson who has been received into a journeyman organization

Compagnonnage (literally, "journeymanship"): From *compagnon*, journeyman. Both the journeyman world as a whole and individual journeyman organizations

Conduite: Ceremony in which members of the journeyman community briefly accompany aspirants departing their city. When the Tour de France was still made on foot, this was a way of paying homage to brothers who had completed their *devoirs*

Dame-hôtesse (lady-hostess): Woman who keeps a journeyman chapter house but has not yet been received as a *mère*

Devoir (literally, "obligation"): *Compagnonnage* itself as well as the totality of its rites, rules, and traditions. Historically, it predates the word *compagnonnage*, which is of nineteenth-century origin

Devoirant: Any journeyman of the *devoir*

Devoir de liberté: Rite officially founded in 1804 acknowledging Solomon as its founder and protector. Membership consists of *loups, indiens,* and *gavots*

Finished journeyman: A *compagnon* who has attained the third level of *compagnonnage,* a status officially conferred in a ceremony of *finition*

Finition (completion): Ceremony in which a journeyman officially reaches the third level of *compagnonnage*

Gavots: Nickname of journeyman joiners and locksmiths of the *devoir de liberté.* On the origins of this term, see p. 106

House (*maison*): Journeyman chapter, to members of the *devoir*

Indiens (Indians): Nickname of journeyman carpenters of the *devoir de liberté*

Interdit de boutique (shop strike): The condemnation of a shop or workshop due to disagreements with the master. When issued, *compagnons* refuse to work in or for the shop in question until the workers' demands are met

Lapin (rabbit): Nickname of apprentice carpenters

Levageur: Contractor-hoister

Livret d'ouvrier (worker's registration book): Under Napoleon, a booklet all journeymen were obliged to carry and update in order for authorities to better track workers' movements and activities

Loup (wolf): Nickname of journeyman stonecutters, children of Solomon. Those in the *devoir* are known as *loups-garous* ("werewolves" or "surly fellows"); journeyman carpenters of the *devoir de liberté* are sometimes called *loups*

Mère (mother): Woman who runs a journeyman chapter; the chapter itself

Passant (itinerant or wayfarer): Journeyman stonecutters, carpenters, roofers, and plasterers of the *devoir*

Pays: Term used by aspirants and journeymen to designate one another (journeymen do not call one another *Monsieur*)

Premier en ville (first in the city): In certain craft fellowships, the journeyman responsible for his society in a given city

Prévôté (provostship): Provincial chapter of the Association Ouvrière des Compagnons du Devoir. The journeyman in charge is known as the *prévôt* (provost)

Province (province): Within the Association Ouvrière, a geographic region encompassing several *prévôtés*

Reception (*réception*): The ritual induction ceremony of an aspirant or affiliate as a *compagnon*

Remarque: A specific piece of information, a landmark, or a monument with which *compagnons* must be familiar in order to prove their passage through a city on the Tour de France

Renard (fox): Nickname of an apprentice in a specific craft, or of anyone not belonging to the journeyman world

Rôle or *Rolle:* The roll or membership list of a journeyman society

Rouleur: Journeyman responsible for receiving and placing newly arrived journeymen, issuing *levages d'acquit* (the official discharge from a city), organizing *conduites* and assemblies, assuring that the organization operates smoothly, and presiding over journeyman festivals and banquets. The *rouleur* always marches at the head of processions

Trait: The art of delineating volumes in depth. Journeyman carpenters, joiners, stonecutters, metalworkers, and tinkers regard learning the *trait* as central to their training

Selected Bibliography

Barret, Pierre, and J.-N. Gurgand. *Ils voyageaient la France: Vie et traditions des compagnons du Tour de France au XIXe siècle.* Paris: Hachette, 1980.

Bayard, Jean-Pierre. *Le Compagnonnage en France.* Paris: Payot, 1978.

Benoist, Luc. *Le Compagnonnage et les métiers.* Paris: Presses universitaires de France, 1966.

Boileau, Étienne. *Le Livre des métiers.* Ed. by René de Lespinasse and François Bonnardot. Paris: 1879.

Boyer, Abel. *La Tour de France d'un compagnon du devoir.* Paris: Librairie du compagnonnage, 1975.

Briquet, Jean. *Agricol Perdiguier: Compagnon du Tour de France et représentant du peuple (1805–1875).* Paris: Éditions de la Butte aux Cailles, 1981.

Cacérès, Bénigno. *Le Compagnon charpentier de Nazareth.* Paris: Éditions du Seuil, 1981.

———. *Regard sur les métiers du bâtiment.* Paris: Éditions du Seuil, 1955.

Coldstream, Nicola. *Masons and Sculptors.* London: British Museum Press, 1991.

Coornaert, Émile. *Le Compagnonnage en France: Du moyen âge à nos jours.* Paris: Éditions ouvrières, 1966.

Davis, Natalie Zemon. *Society and Culture in Early Modern France.* Stanford, Calif.: Stanford University Press, 1975.

Dubreuil, Hyacinthe. *Promotion.* Paris: Éditions de l'Entreprise Moderne, 1963.

———. *Le Travail et la civilisation.* Paris: Plon, 1953.

Dughet, M. *Mémoires d'une mère en devoir.* Paris: Librairie du compagnonnage, 1979.

Edeline, René. *Les Compagnons du tour de France.* Paris: Imprimerie Brodard et Taupin, 1964.

Erlande-Brandenburg, Alain. *Cathedrals and Castles: Building in the Middle Ages.* New York: Abrams, 1995.

Hauser, Henri. *Les Compagnons d'arts et métiers à Dijon.* Paris: Éditions Laffitte, 1980.

Icher, François. *Building the Great Cathedrals.* New York: Abrams, 1998.

———. *Le Compagnonnage.* Paris: Éditions Jacques Grancher, 1989.

Lambert, René. *La Sainte-Baume, le pèlerinage des compagnons du devoir.* Paris: Librairie du compagnonnage, 1997.

Langlois, Émile (Émile, le Normand). *Compagnon du devoir.* Paris: Flammarion, 1983.

Lecotté, Roger. *Archives historiques du compagnonnage.* Paris: Mémoires de la Fédération Folklorique de l'Île-de-France, 1956.

———. *Chefs-d'oeuvre de compagnons.* Paris: Éditions Chêne-Hachette, 1980.

———. "Essai bibliographique sur les compagnonnages de tous les devoirs de Tour de France." *Compagnonnage: Par les compagnons du Tour de France.* Ed. by Raoul Dautry. Paris: Éditions Laffitte, 1951.

Mackey, Albert G. *The History of Freemasonry: The Legendary Origins.* 1898. Reprint, New York: Grammercy, 1996.

Martin Saint-Léon, E. *Le Compagnonnage.* Paris: Librairie du compagnonnage, 1977.

Ménétra, Jacques-Louis. *Journal of My Life.* Ed. by Daniel Roche, trans. by Arthur Goldhammer. New York: Columbia University Press, 1986.

Perdiguier, Agricol. *Le Livre du compagnonnage.* 1839. Reprint, Paris: Éditions Laffitte, 1981.

———. *Mémoires d'un compagnon.* Ed. by Alain Faure. Paris: Librairie du compagnonnage, 1977.

Sand, George. *Le Compagnon du tour de France.* 1841. Reprint, Paris: J.C.M., 1979.

Sewell, William H., Jr. *Work and Revolution in France: The Language of Labor from the Old Regime to 1848.* Cambridge: Cambridge University Press, 1980.

Sonenscher, Michael. *The Hatters of Eighteenth-Century France.* Berkeley, Calif.: Berkeley University Press, 1987.

Truant, Cynthia Maria. *The Rites of Labor: Brotherhoods of Compagnonnage in Old and New Regime France.* Ithaca, N.Y., and London: Cornell University Press, 1994.

Vergez, Raoul. *Les Compagnons d'aujourd'hui.* Paris: 1973.

———. *La Pendule à Salomon.* Paris: Presses Pocket, 1983.

Vincenot, Henri. *The Prophet of Compostela: A Novel of Apprenticeship and Initiation.* Trans. by E. E. Rehmus. Rochester, Vt.: Inner Traditions International, 1996.

Zdatny, Steven. *The Politics of Survival: Artisans in Twentieth-Century France.* Oxford: Oxford University Press.

Index

Photograph Credits